MORTGAGE CLUB

TIM RHEY &
RICH HANLIN

Copyright Page

Mortgage Club
12 Rules They Don't Want You to Know –
The Underground Guide to Never Getting Hustled Again.

For permission requests, contact:
Email: Tim@trueratemortgagegroup.com

First Edition, 2025
Printed in the United States of America

Disclaimer

This book is intended for informational and educational purposes only. The content represents the opinions and experiences of the authors and should not be considered financial, legal, tax, or investment advice. Mortgage products, rates, guidelines, and lending regulations change frequently, and the strategies discussed may not apply to every situation. Readers should consult with a licensed mortgage professional, attorney, financial advisor, or tax professional before making any decisions.

This book is not a commitment to lend, extend credit, or make any specific loan program or interest rate available. All loans are subject to credit approval, underwriting guidelines, and other qualifications. Information is believed to be accurate at the time of publication but is not guaranteed.

Names, characters, and scenarios may have been changed for privacy, illustrative purposes, or storytelling clarity.

Any resemblance to actual persons, living or dead, is purely coincidental.

Licensing Information

Tim Rhey, NMLS #883312

Rich Hanlin, NMLS #263188

Xpert Home Lending Inc, NMLS:2179191 DRE:02166758, Xpert Home Lending is an Equal Housing Lender.

This isn't a mortgage book.
It's a rebellion against
the status quo.

Read This Before You Get Played

This isn't a sales pitch.

It's a warning.

We've watched too many smart people get blindsided by a system built to confuse them.

We've sat across from first-time buyers who trusted the wrong advice.

We've cleaned up messes left by lazy lenders.

We've watched families sign loan papers they didn't understand—because nobody gave them the playbook.

That's what ***Mortgage Club*** is: The unfiltered manual to beating the system before it beats you.

So why listen to us?

Tim Rhey is the founder of True Rate Mortgage Group and author of First Mortgage 101. For nearly two decades, he's helped buyers cut through the noise, structure smart loans, and win the mortgage game.

Rich Hanlin is the President of Xpert Home Lending, a 35-year mortgage veteran, and one of the top 10 national brokers for eight straight years. His mission? Make homeownership achievable—and fix a broken industry along the way.

We've closed thousands of deals.

We've been behind the curtain.

And we're here to tell you: this game can be won.

But only if you know the rules.

This book gives you those rules.

The 12 no-fluff laws of mortgage combat.

The secrets they don't want you to know.

The edge you need to walk in confident—and walk out a homeowner.

Let's go.

Welcome to Mortgage Club.

Table of Contents

Introduction

Something's wrong with the way people are buying homes today.

The pressure. The confusion. The gut check that says,

"This doesn't feel right . . . but I guess this is how it works?"

We wrote this book because we couldn't keep watching good people—families, first-timers, the hopeful and the hardworking—get handed a raw deal and smile through it like they just didn't know better.

We've closed thousands of loans.
We've seen behind the curtain.
And we're here to tell you:

The game is winnable.
But only if you know the rules.

Mortgage Club is your playbook to overcoming these limitations.

We want to level the playing field.

The goal of this book is to transform the average, unprepared homebuyer into a confident, well-armed borrower who knows the rules of the mortgage game—and how to win.

Twelve rules. One mission.

Help you buy smart, borrow wisely, and never get played again.

It's part mortgage manual, part war guide, and part wake-up call for anyone who's ever nodded their way through a closing they didn't fully understand.

You deserve better.
And we're here to give it to you—straight up, no filter, no fake smiles.

Ever seen *Fight Club*?
Remember Rule #1?

Don't talk about Fight Club?

Yeah. We're breaking that one.
Because in Mortgage Club, we talk.

We spill the secrets.
We shine lights where others won't.
And we do it with a little humor, a little grit, and a whole lot of heart.

This book will teach you:

- How to spot garbage loan advice from a mile away
- How to keep thousands in your pocket at closing
- How to negotiate like a pro—even if it's your first time
- How to think like an investor, even if you're not one
- How to walk into any mortgage meeting with total confidence
- How to think like an underwriter and improve your approval odds

But we didn't write this book to be edgy.
We wrote it because we care.

Rich runs Xpert Home Lending, one of the largest broker shops in the business. Tim leads True Rate, a company built on helping borrowers navigate the process with clarity and confidence.

We're not just lending experts—we're husbands. Dads. Neighbors.
We've been on both sides of the desk.

We know how overwhelming this all can feel when it's your first time . . .
or your third time . . .
or your last shot at finally owning something real.

This book is for people like you.

If you're tired of being in the dark . . .
If you want the tools, the mindset, and the knowledge to win . . .
Then you're in the right place.

This is the underground guide for the people who actually give a damn.

The ones who aren't afraid to ask questions.
The ones who want more for their families.
The ones who refuse to be another mortgage horror story.

Welcome to Mortgage Club.

It's not always polite.
It's not always pretty.
But it's the truth.

And it might just save you a whole lot of money—and years of regret.

Lace 'em up. Let's move.

—Tim & Rich

RULE #1:

Don't Get Sold.
Get Smart.

Mortgage Club Confession: The $15,000 Thank-You That Almost Cost Him $48,000

-By Tim Rhey

A few years ago, I had a client—great guy, super sharp, family man. Let's call him Brian.

Brian was halfway through the loan process with us when he decided to wander into a shiny new construction model home. You know the kind—clean lines, fresh paint smell, open-concept dreams.

He calls me later that afternoon, absolutely buzzing.

"Tim, you're not gonna believe this—the builder's lender is offering me $15,000 in closing cost credits if I go with them! I mean . . . that's free money. I'd be crazy not to take it, right?"

Now, pause right there.

Let's acknowledge something: $15,000 is a head-turner. And to his credit, Brian wasn't trying to be shady. He was calling me because he felt guilty. Like he was breaking up with someone over text, and I'd just been blindsided with "It's not you, it's the builder's lender."

So I did what I always do—no guilt trip, no hard sell.
I simply said, "Brian, that does sound amazing. But before you make the switch, do me one favor—just send over their Loan

Estimate. Let me take a look. If it's truly free money, I'll tell you to take it, and I'll be the first to toast you at closing."

What happened next is exactly why this story needs to be told.

Because when I opened that Loan Estimate . . . my jaw didn't drop—it dislocated.

Buried in the details was a $15,000 "Discount Fee."
Let that sink in. They weren't giving him $15,000. They were adding that $15,000 to the loan in the form of additional fees.

Not only that, but the rate they were offering him was 0.5% higher than what we had already locked in for him. Over the life of the loan, that "free gift" was going to cost him $48,000 more in interest. And the worst part? He had no idea.

So I called Brian.

I calmly walked him through the statement line by line. Patient. No drama. On the other end of the line, I could hear it happening in real time . . . The Five Stages of Mortgage Grief.

1. Denial: "No way. They said it was free money. That can't be right."
2. Anger: "Are you kidding me?! They lied to me?"
3. Bargaining: "Maybe if I talk to them . . . maybe they can drop the fee?"
4. Depression: "Man, I almost signed this. I was literally ready to leave you guys."

5. Acceptance: "Tim . . . thank you. You just saved me. I'm staying with you. Let's finish this thing."

And we did. We closed on time. No gimmicks, no smoke and mirrors, no "free money" with strings attached. Just the truth. The real numbers. The right deal.

• • • • • • • • • • • • • • •

There's no such thing as free money in a mortgage. If it sounds too good to be true . . . it's probably already hidden in your interest rate or your fees. Builders don't give—they recover.

If I had a dollar for every time a builder's lender dangled "free closing costs" like candy, I wouldn't be writing this—I'd be running ads for them. But I don't. Because I actually read the label. I do the math. I protect my clients.

And Brian?

He learned a lesson that day—not about mortgages, but about people.
And he's still a client to this day.

Because once you know who's really in your corner . . . you don't forget it.

You've seen *Fight Club*, right?

The first rule of Fight Club is: You do not talk about Fight Club.

But this isn't Fight Club. This is Mortgage Club—where we knock out confusing offers and marketing hype so you get the best rate and fees.

Think Tyler Durden meets Warren Buffett—ready to fight the hype while protecting your wallet.

So what's the first rule of Mortgage Club?

Don't get sold. Get smart.

Because here's the truth that no one taught you in school:

Your mortgage isn't a trophy. It's not a reward for being responsible. It's a product.

And like any product, it's being sold.

We're not here to paint lenders as villains. Heck, we are lenders. But you need to know the truth:

Lenders get paid when you close.
They make more when you borrow more.
They get paid faster if you don't ask questions.

That doesn't make them evil.
It just means you need to be smarter.

Because you're not just buying a home.
You're buying the loan that pays for it.

If you don't understand that deal?
You'll pay for it for the next 30 years.

The Mindset Shift: You're Buying a Loan, Not Just a Home

This is where most buyers go wrong.

They fall in love with the house—the open floor plan, the big backyard, the kitchen island.
But they forget: The loan pays for all of it.

Your loan is the real purchase.
That monthly payment decides what you can save. Where you vacation. What you invest in.

It's not just money leaving your account. It's your life after the purchase.

Yet, most people spend more time comparing paint colors than they do comparing lenders.

We see it every day.
Smart, educated people who know every school district in town—but don't know what "origination fees" even mean.

It's not their fault.
No one teaches this in school.

We've seen families who moved here from other countries with nothing.
They work three jobs. Pool money with relatives. Put ten people in one house.
Why?

Because they want something that's theirs.
They know what ownership means.
They know it's the first step toward generational wealth.

Meanwhile, too many Americans avoid buying because they're afraid of debt—while renting for decades and paying someone else's mortgage.

We get it.
Debt can be scary.

But here's the difference:
Smart debt builds wealth.
Dumb debt builds regret.

Mortgage Club exists to make sure you know the difference.

Why Lenders Aren't Your Enemy (But Aren't Your Best Friend Either)

We're going to be straight with you:

Lenders have goals.
Their business model is to make money on interest, fees,

and volume.
They have overhead, staff, sometimes shareholders.

They're not giving out loans because they like you. They're managing risk—and trying to profit from it.

That's not evil.
That's business.

But here's what buyers often forget:

It's your job to make sure you're getting the best deal for you.

Because no lender is going to say:
"Hey, wait. You could actually pay us less if you negotiated."

That's not their job.
It's yours.

We want you to understand that so you don't mistake being polite for being prepared.

Ownership changes everything.

We've both seen this firsthand.

Neighborhoods that were once so bad you couldn't give a house away are now million-dollar ZIP codes.

Ownership shifts the dynamic.

It stabilizes communities.
It builds equity.
It gives families a foundation.

That's what homeownership is really about.

Legacy.
Security.
Changing the trajectory of a family.

But here's the thing:
Wanting the dream isn't enough.
You have to understand the deal that gets you there.

How the Sales Pitch Works

If you've shopped for a mortgage, you know the lines:

"Lowest rates ever!"
"No closing costs!"
"You're approved for $700,000!"

It's designed to make you feel excited. Safe. Grateful.

But here's the reality:

"Lowest rates ever" might assume you're putting 40% down, have an 850 credit score, and are paying thousands in discount points.

"No closing costs" usually means you're paying a higher rate for decades.

"Approved for $700,000" isn't your budget—it's the lender's risk tolerance.

It's marketing.
It's sales.
It's not personal.
But it is planned.

They know you're emotional.
They know you're imagining holiday dinners and backyard BBQs.
They know you're exhausted from house hunting.

So they give you a simple pitch:
Just sign.

But if you don't slow down and ask questions?
You're buying a payment you might regret.

Because confusion is profitable.

Trust but verify.

We're not saying don't trust anyone.
We're saying:

Ask questions.
Don't rush.

Because lenders respect borrowers who know what they want.

The ones who get pressured to sign quickly?
They're the ones paying the most.

Fees, Rates, and the Real Math

Let's talk numbers.

According to the CFPB, closing costs usually run 2–5% of the home price.
On a $400,000 home, that's $8,000–$20,000.
Not exactly pocket change.

And these costs?

They're not always labeled clearly.
They can hide in:

- Processing fees
- Underwriting fees
- Doc prep fees
- Admin fees

Some are legit.
Some are negotiable.
Some are pure profit.

> "The loan is the real product.
> The house is just the wrapper."

Discount Points

"Discount points" sounds smart.

Pay upfront to lower your rate.
But is it really smart for you?

Sometimes yes.
Sometimes it's paying $5,000 now to save $10 a month for 30 years.

Always do the math.
Because no one else is going to do it for you.

Interest Rates Aren't One Number

This one kills us.

People think there's a single "best rate" out there. There isn't.

Rates change daily.
They depend on your credit score, debt-to-income ratio, loan-to-value, property type, loan type, and loan term.
They also often include baked-in costs you don't see at first glance.

We've seen lenders advertise rock-bottom rates. But by the time you call?

The market has moved.
Or that rate is for someone with perfect credit paying five points upfront.

Here's a real stat:

Freddie Mac found that getting just one extra quote saves borrowers an average of $1,500.
Getting three quotes? Average savings jumps to $3,500.

Same house.
Same borrower.
Totally different outcome.

Just because they shopped.

RULE #2:

Credit Is Armor. Don't Show Up Defenseless.

Mortgage Club Confession: Jacqueline's Blindfolded Offer

By Rich Hanlin

Let me tell you a story that still rattles me every time I think about it.

A woman named Jacqueline came to me for a pre-approval. Pretty normal, right? Except there was one major problem . . .

She'd already made an offer on a home.

Let me be crystal clear: She was already under contract, and her realtor was now asking for a pre-approval letter to back it up—after the fact.

That's like walking into a courtroom and asking for a lawyer after the verdict. I'd never worked with her before. We were total strangers. A friend had given her my info and told her that I "knew what I was doing." I guess that was enough.

So I pulled her credit.

Her score was borderline. Technically high enough for a manual underwrite on an FHA loan, which is very different from a standard FHA approval. Manual underwriting means more scrutiny, stricter limits, and way less wiggle room.

She also wanted down payment assistance—a program with even more restrictions.

And then I saw the real landmines: open charge-offs, accounts she claimed belonged to her daughter. A car loan that she said she had co-signed for, but that her daughter was making the payments on.

From an underwriting standpoint, it didn't matter. The debts were in her name.

Here I was, being asked to issue a pre-approval to back up a signed offer for a borrower whose financial profile didn't yet support it.

Now I'm part of it.

Now I'm the one holding up the seller.

Now I'm the guy everyone's waiting on.

To make a long story short, we got it closed—barely.

We ditched the down payment assistance and pivoted to a regular FHA loan, which allowed higher debt ratios. I added the daughter as a co-borrower. And thankfully, Jacqueline and her husband had $26,000 in the bank—they just didn't want to use it. That saved the deal. If they hadn't had that reserve? I would've pulled the plug immediately.

• • • • • • • • • • • • • • •

But here's the million-dollar question:

If Jacqueline had known her credit situation before making that offer . . . would she have made it?

Probably not.

She got lucky.

She found someone like me—someone who's been doing this for 35+ years and knows how to maneuver the system when the walls close in.

But most borrowers? They wouldn't be so fortunate.

They'd get denied. They'd lose the home.

They'd leave a seller hanging. And the whole deal would collapse in frustration and regret.

Here's the lesson:

Credit is your armor—not your afterthought.

Before you make an offer, before you tour homes, before your realtor starts writing contracts—know where you score.

Because in this business, blind offers break deals.

And if I didn't know what I was doing—or if she hadn't had money tucked away?

That deal never would've closed.

And Jacqueline would've learned her lesson the hard way.

You should never walk into a fight without knowing the weapons and resources at your disposal. At least not if you are wise.

So why would you walk into a mortgage negotiation without knowing your credit?

Your credit is your armor.

It's your advantage.

It's the difference between winning a great deal and getting pummeled with fees and interest for decades.

The Mindset Shift: Credit Is Strategy, Not Shame

A lot of people treat their credit score like it's a confession booth.

"I don't want to look."

"I'm embarrassed."

"Let's just see what the lender says."

That's the wrong approach.

Your credit score is not your moral worth.

It's not proof you're good or bad.

It's a tool.

A number that says, "How risky is it to lend you money?"

Lenders don't care about your life story.

They care about whether you'll pay them back.

So don't make it emotional.

Make it strategic.

Why Credit Matters So Much

Credit matters differently depending on the deal. Buying a million-dollar house? You'd better prove you can handle a million-dollar obligation. Buying a $150,000 condo? The bar is different—but it's still there. Lenders want proof. Proof you can handle debt responsibly. Proof you've paid other creditors on time. They typically want to see:

At least two accounts with 24 months of history

At least one account with 12 months

That's the bare minimum.

And what kind of accounts? Not student loans in deferral. Not closed credit cards from ten years ago. They want active, current credit showing on-time payments. Some people proudly say, "I paid off everything and closed all my accounts." That's great for your personal discipline—but terrible for lending. No open accounts means no scorable credit.

Rent, utilities, and cell phones can help document responsibility, but they don't generate a FICO score on their own. They can sometimes be added to meet minimum requirements, but they don't replace real credit history. You can't work down to qualify. You have to build up your credit profile.

It's Not About Cash

A common objection goes like this: "I have half a million in the bank. Why does my credit matter?" We get it. But cash and credit aren't the same. Cash shows you have money now. Credit shows you pay your debts over time.

Lenders don't care if you have money under the mattress. You're not buying the house with cash—you're asking them to front the money.

They want to know if you're good for it.

What's the risk you won't pay them back?

You wouldn't loan a friend $500,000 just because he says, "Trust me," right? Same thing here.

Secrets from Underwriting: How Lenders Really Look at Credit

Underwriters don't just look at your score. They look at your credit profile. They want to see how you manage debt.

Do you have open, active trade lines?

Do you pay on time over the last 12 to 24 months?

Do you have enough history to trust?

Some borrowers think, "I have no debt, so I'm perfect." But no credit history at all? That's just as risky to a lender as bad credit.

No credit means no evidence.

Lenders want data. Rent, utilities, cell phones—those are helpful to prove you pay bills. But they don't generate scorable credit by themselves. Those can be added manually for thin credit files, but they don't replace true revolving or installment accounts.

Bottom line?

You can't cheat the system by removing everything. You have to build it up.

> *"Credit isn't a reflection of who you are. It's a reflection of how ready you are."*

Building Credit from Scratch or After Damage

We hear it all the time.

"I don't have any credit."

"I'm rebuilding after bankruptcy."

"No one will give me a card to get started."

It's the classic catch-22: you need credit to get credit. But there is a path: secured credit cards. You put down $200 to $500 as collateral. The bank lends you your own money, charges you interest, and reports your payments. Sounds silly? It works. That's how many people rebuild after financial setbacks. It's exactly how some of us rebuilt our own credit after the 2008 crash.

Here's how to do it right. Get the secured card. Use it every month. Buy something small, maybe a tank of gas, a pair of socks. Wait for the statement. Pay it off in full. That shows real, scorable usage.

Most people think, "I'll get it but never use it." Wrong. You need to use credit to prove you can handle it. Lenders want to see activity and repayment. That's the whole game. Once you establish the basics, you can add things like rent or utilities to your credit profile. But first? You need scorable, revolving or installment accounts.

How Credit Scores Really Work

Let's bust a big myth right now: There's no single, secret formula that works for everyone.

Credit scoring is complicated because everyone's profile is different.

Different limits.

Different histories.

Different account types.

But there are universal truths.

One big factor is utilization. Imagine all your credit cards combined have $25,000 in available credit. If you owe $20,000 total, you're using 80 percent. That's high.

For the best scores, you usually want to be below 50 percent—even better, under 30 percent. And it's not just about your total utilization. Each individual card matters, too. If you're maxed out on one card but another is empty, that still drags your score down. Scoring models see how you manage each line.

Credit scoring looks at:

- How much you owe overall
- How much you owe on each card
- How often you use it
- How you pay it back

It even notices big changes. Just bought a car for $80,000? Your credit might dip temporarily because it's adjusting to that new debt, even if you've always paid on time.

We've seen so many clients say, "But I've always paid on time!"

Fantastic.

But if you're carrying big balances, your score still suffers.

Your credit is alive.

It changes with your behavior.

Easy Ways to Improve Quickly

This isn't theory. We do this for clients every single day. We'll pull their credit report and figure out the cheapest, fastest way to raise their score to the level they need. Not 800+. Just enough to get the best loan program.

Example:

A client comes in with a 550 score. They need 620 to qualify for an FHA with 3.5 percent down. So, we analyze the report: "Pay this card down $1,200. Clear this small collection. That's it."

It's targeted.

It's efficient.

Because your score isn't magic.

It's math.

The Three-Bureau Reality

Mortgage lenders pull all three credit bureaus.

Equifax.
TransUnion.
Experian.

And they don't use the average. They use the middle score. If your scores are 750, 680, and 620? They toss the high and the low. You're a 680.

Some people get misled by watching just one score.

"But Credit Karma says I'm 740!"

Great.

But if the other scores are trash, you're not getting that rate.

Reports can differ between bureaus because:

- Some creditors only report to one or two
- Some debts only show up on certain reports
- Errors can exist on just one

That's why you have to fix all three.

If you pay off a collection on TransUnion, but it's still on Equifax and Experian? You didn't fix the problem. You just did a third of the work. We've seen people lose their dream home because they didn't realize they needed to clean up all three reports.

Don't let that be you.

How to Pull and Review Your Reports

Don't rely on Credit Karma. Don't rely on free scores from your bank. Use AnnualCreditReport.com. It's federally guaranteed. You get all three reports free once per year.

Print them.

Read them carefully.

Highlight errors.

Note accounts that don't belong to you.

Check addresses and names.

Your credit is your borrowing resume. If it's got junk on it, clean it up.

Common Errors (and How to Fix Them)

Credit reports are notorious for mistakes. We've seen everything—family members with the same name getting mixed up, Juniors and Seniors ending up with each other's debts, even accounts that don't belong to the borrower at all. We once helped a buyer whose score tanked because his dad's credit cards showed up on his report. Same name. Different Social. Still got merged.

Fixing it isn't rocket science. You prove it's not yours. Provide statements, ID, and address history. Challenge it with the bureau. They're legally required to investigate. It's not instant—but it works. And remember, you have to fix it on all three bureaus. Don't assume one fix cleans them all.

We've also seen deals die at the closing table because the title search found liens the buyer didn't disclose. One borrower lied about not owing child support. The lien didn't show in his local county, but it popped up when they searched old addresses. Result? $180,000 in unpaid support. Deal dead on the spot.

It's not just the credit bureaus watching. Title companies run deep searches. Creditors file liens the moment they see that you own property. Once you own real estate, your debt becomes a target. Those creditors will wait years to get their payday—and they will.

Real Talk About Collections

Collections don't always have to be paid before you buy. Lenders will often just count 5 percent of the balance against your monthly debt ratio. So if you owe $10,000 in collections, they'll treat it like a $500 monthly payment. If your ratios can handle it, you might close without paying it off.

But they're not gone. Those creditors know you own an asset now. They will file liens to get paid when you refinance or sell. You can't outrun them forever. It's better to face it up front—and on your terms.

How to Beat the System: Action Steps

We're not here to scare you.

We're here to arm you.

Here's the Mortgage Club plan:

1. Pull your credit reports annually. Use AnnualCreditReport.com.

2. Review every line. Are those accounts yours? Are the balances accurate?
3. Fix what's wrong. Dispute errors in writing. Provide proof.
4. Build a real credit profile. Get secured cards. Use them monthly.
5. Mind your utilization. Stay below 50 percent per card—30 percent is better.
6. Plan early. Credit repair takes time. Don't wait until you need it.

We want you to walk into the lender's office with confidence. Not hoping for approval. Expecting the best terms—because you've done the work.

Pro Tips

- Check all three bureaus.
- Be patient but persistent.
- Think like an underwriter.
- Build credit before you need it.
- Keep accounts open.
- Stay consistent.

We want you to walk in like you own the place. Because when you do the prep, you kind of do.

Quick Recap

- Your credit is your armor.
- It's not shame—it's strategy.
- Lenders use it to judge risk.
- Errors are common—fix them.
- Build credit before you need it.
- Check all three bureaus.
- Keep balances low.
- Use credit smartly and pay on time.

Reader Challenge

Pull your credit this week.

Get all three reports.

Highlight one thing you can fix or improve.

Make a plan to do it.

Closing Pep Talk

We know this isn't the fun part of buying a home. It's way more fun to pick out kitchen cabinets and dream about backyard barbecues.

But the truth is, your credit is the real key to the front door. It decides the rate you get, the fees you pay, and the monthly payment you'll live with for decades.

If you want the best deal, the best payment, the best stability for your family? You have to earn it with preparation. This isn't about being perfect. It's about being smart.

At Mortgage Club, we don't get sold.

We get prepared.

And we fight for the deal we deserve.

Welcome to the club.

Bonus Section: Advanced Moves & Game Plan

- Get a secured card if you're rebuilding. Use it monthly. Pay in full.
- Add rent or utilities to your credit reports to document payment history.
- Plan for all three bureaus. Fix errors across all of them.
- Mind utilization. Stay under 50 percent per card. Under 30 percent is better.
- Schedule a credit review before you shop for homes to avoid last-minute surprises.

Because knowing your credit is your armor.

And you don't go into battle unprepared.

RULE #3:

Budget Like a Boss. Not a Bank Puppet.

Mortgage Club Confession: Elizabeth vs. the Limit

-By Tim Rhey

Let me tell you a story about a client I'll never forget. We'll call her Elizabeth.

Fresh out of college, high GPA, high-paying job, no student loans—a unicorn, really. She landed a great role in computer engineering and had the world at her feet. A sharp woman with zero debt and a six-figure salary before age 25. She had her future mapped out like an algorithm.

But Elizabeth was on a mission. To prove something. To someone.
Maybe to the world . . . maybe to herself. But the pressure was there—quiet, unspoken, and real.

When we first connected, she told me confidently, "Tim, I want my mortgage payment around $2,000 a month. That's what I'm comfortable with."

"Perfect," I said. "We'll keep everything within that zone."

And for a while . . . we did.

But then something changed.

As she started shopping, that $2,000 target slowly began to blur. The houses got bigger. The neighborhoods got fancier. And the budget? It started creeping up like a slow leak in a tire.

Then came the question I've heard too many times: "What's the maximum I qualify for?"

I gave her the number because that's my job. But I also gave her a caution.

"Just because the bank says you can . . . doesn't mean you should. You were very clear from day one—$2,000 a month was the number. That came from you, not the system."

But the system was louder. The builder. The realtor. Even the shiny kitchen island with quartz counters seemed to whisper, *You can afford this.*

And eventually . . . Elizabeth believed it.

She bought the dream home. Beautiful place. Big yard. Elegant fixtures. A little over budget—well, a lot over budget—but the bank said it was fine.

And about a year later, she called me back.

"Tim . . . is it possible to refinance? The payment is really killing me."

Same job. Same income. No big life changes. But the truth was now painfully obvious:

She didn't buy the house her heart wanted.
She bought the house that the algorithm allowed.
And she was drowning in it.

Not just the mortgage—the cost of living in that home. The heating bill. The yardwork. The burst water heater she never budgeted for. The constant Amazon packages for curtains, furniture, and decor. The HOA fees. The adulting.

And that $2,000 number?

That was the budget her gut gave her. The real one. The one rooted in peace.
Not the pre-approval.
Not the algorithm.
Not the "Congratulations! You're Approved" letter.

• • • • • • • • • • • • • • •

Mortgage Club Confession:

The bank doesn't know your lifestyle. Your sleep patterns. Your vacation goals. Your faith, your family, your future.

Only you know what kind of monthly payment brings peace—and what kind brings panic.
If you let the bank decide your limit, don't be surprised when you find yourself living at it.

Elizabeth got through it. She's doing okay now—learned a hard lesson, the way many do: through stress, regret, and unnecessary pressure.

She told me later, "The worst part wasn't the money . . . it was the noise in my head. Every time I paid that mortgage, I'd hear a voice saying, *You knew better.*"

And she did.

But when you're surrounded by salespeople cheering you into a bigger house and a bigger loan, it takes strength to say, "No thanks—I'll take peace instead."

Elizabeth knows that now.
And so do you.

Why This Rule Saves You Years of Stress

We want to talk about something real for a minute.
Not just the math.
Not just the payment.

The weight of an unaffordable mortgage is suffocating.

It's the argument with your spouse when you admit there's no money for a vacation this year.
It's the 2 a.m. stare-down with your bank account, wondering if the lights will stay on.
It's the debate about groceries versus the credit card minimum.

We've seen couples who were perfect for each other get absolutely wrecked by money stress.

We've watched families sacrifice time together because one parent had to pick up a second job.
We've seen clients look exhausted, worn down, and feeling trapped.

When you stretch to the very limit of your budget, you don't just sign a mortgage contract—you sign away options.

You give up flexibility.
You lose the freedom to pivot when life changes.

It's easy to think: *We'll make it work.*
We'll cut back.
We'll adjust.

But most people don't.
Or they do, but at the cost of their happiness and peace.

We're not here to scare you out of buying.
We're here to tell you that a home should support your life—not swallow it whole.

This rule isn't about telling you "no."
It's about giving you permission to say "enough."

Enough house to be safe.
Enough room to live well.
But not so much that you can't breathe.

Let's Walk Through the Math

Let's make this painfully real.

Say you're paying $2,500 a month in rent now.
It's tight, but you're making it.

Your lender says:
"Great news! You're pre-approved up to $4,000 a month!"

What does that jump actually mean?

$1,500 more every month.
$18,000 more a year.
For 30 years.

Can you find $18,000 in your current budget?

Where's it coming from?
Eating out?
Vacations?
Your kid's soccer?
Your retirement contributions?

And that's before you factor in property taxes, insurance, and maintenance.

Example Breakdown

$2,500/month rent → Mortgage at $4,000/month might include:

- $2,800 principal & interest
- $600 property taxes
- $300 homeowners' insurance
- $300 mortgage insurance (if <20% down)

But that's the starting point.
Bigger house? Higher taxes. More expensive insurance.
More to heat, cool, and maintain.

We want you to see it in black and white.
Because when you do, you can choose wisely.

"The wrong loan doesn't just cost you money—it costs you momentum, peace of mind, and the chance to build wealth on your terms."

Debt-to-Income Ratios: The Details Banks Don't Explain

Banks love debt-to-income ratios.
They look clean.
They feel official.

But let's break them down.

Most loan programs use two ratios:

- **Front-end DTI**: Housing payment divided by gross income
- **Back-end DTI**: Total debts (housing + credit cards + car loans + student loans) divided by gross income

Common lender maxes?

- 43–50% back-end DTI, depending on the loan program
- FHA, VA, and certain conventional loans might go higher with "compensating factors"

Sounds fine on paper.
But let's do real math.

If you gross $10,000/month and get approved at 50% DTI, that's $5,000 a month in total debt payments.

But after taxes, you might only bring home $7,000.

Now you've got $5,000 in debts . . . and $2,000 left for everything else:

- Food
- Gas
- Childcare
- Health insurance
- Utilities
- Emergencies

- Entertainment

That's the trap.
Gross income doesn't buy groceries.

Professional Insight: How Lenders View You

We want to be real.

Lenders aren't your enemy.
But they're not your best friend either.

Their job is to get you approved within guidelines. To make sure the loan can be sold, insured, or kept on their books.

They are **not** tasked with protecting your lifestyle.

We are.

We are the brokers who are experts in aligning clients with the best lenders for their specific situation.

It's not a one-size-fits-all with us.

We get clients all the time who were recently rejected by a bank or credit union because of a rule or credit overlay. Because banks, credit unions, and many lenders are stuck with limited products and options, they are often unable to help clients. Our system is designed to handle almost any asset, income, or credit challenge our clients face.

We ask you the questions no underwriter will:

- Do you have savings for emergencies?
- Are you planning for kids?
- How stable is your job?
- Do you rely on bonuses or overtime?
- How much do you want to travel?
- What will make you lose sleep at night?

Because a good mortgage plan isn't just about "yes or no."
It's about how you'll feel living with the answer.

The Reality Conversation

We tell our clients:
Don't just look at the approval letter. Look at your life.

How much are you paying now?
How does that payment feel?

If you're paying $2,500 in rent and that already feels tight . . .
What happens at $4,000?

Is it worth losing date nights?
Family trips?
Your sense of financial safety?

We ask every buyer:
"What does your last 60–90 days of spending actually look like?"

Most people don't know.

They have no idea how much goes to:

- Starbucks
- Amazon
- DoorDash
- Target runs

It's death by a thousand cuts.

We don't judge.

We don't tell you to stop living.

We just want you to **know**.

Buying a house is the biggest financial commitment most people ever make. It deserves that level of honesty.

Lifestyle Inflation: The Silent Killer

Another truth: It's not just the mortgage payment.

Bigger house = bigger bills.

- Higher property taxes
- Higher insurance
- More furniture
- More rooms to heat and cool
- More maintenance

We see it over and over:

Buyers stretch for the max price . . .
Then go shopping to "fill the space."

- Brand new couches
- Big-screen TVs for every room
- Smart home upgrades
- Deck furniture
- Landscaping

Suddenly, the payment isn't the only thing bleeding them dry.

And the worst part?

They tell themselves they deserve it.

That they're building a dream.

That it's the American way.

We're not saying you shouldn't enjoy your home. We're saying: **Know the full cost before you commit.**

Real Talk About Maintenance and Repairs

Let's talk about something no one loves: **maintenance.**

Renters call the landlord.
Homeowners pay the bill.

- New HVAC unit: $6,000-12,000
- Roof replacement: $10,000–$20,000
- Water heater: $1,500
- Plumbing emergency: $500–$5,000

Owning means being responsible for it all.

Your budget needs room for this.

We tell buyers to plan on **1–2% of the home's value annually** for maintenance.

That's $4,000–$8,000 a year on a $400,000 home.

Most people don't plan for it.
Then the first big bill comes—and the credit cards come out.

We don't want that for you.
We want you to be ready.

Hard Questions to Ask Yourself

Ask these before writing an offer:

- Could you handle this payment if one partner lost their job?
- How stable is your industry?
- Are you relying on overtime or bonuses to make the payment?
- Do you have at least 3–6 months of expenses in savings?
- How much do you want left over for vacations, hobbies, and eating out?
- How important is sleeping well at night?

These aren't meant to scare you.
They're meant to **empower** you.

You deserve to buy a home that fits your **real life**—not just your pre-approval letter.

Stories from the Trenches

We've seen it all.

We've seen buyers with eyes bigger than their budgets.

One couple fell in love with a house twice their planned payment.
Their lender said: You qualify. No problem.

They moved in, bought new furniture, and threw a big housewarming party.
Six months later, they were fighting about money every night.
They stopped going out.
Stopped taking trips.
Stopped talking kindly to each other.

They sold the house at a loss a year later, exhausted.

We've also seen the smart buyers.

The couple, who qualified for $4,500/month, chose a home at $3,000.
They kept going on vacations.
Kept funding their retirement.
Had money for home improvements without debt.
They loved their house—and their life.

We've helped clients who didn't realize their $2,500 rent included:

- Utilities they'd never paid before
- HOA fees
- Lawn maintenance
- Water and sewer bills

We had to show them the **real** budget.
Because you can't live in a number on paper.
You live in the **reality of the bill**.

Professional Insight: Broker vs. Bank Conversations

Let's be real about this, too. Not all lenders will have this talk with you. Some banks want you in the biggest loan they can justify. They're looking at commissions, quotas, and volume.

Brokers can be better—but not always.
Some are hustling for numbers.

Others, like us, see our job as telling you the truth.

We'll ask you the uncomfortable questions.
We'll help you see options you might not have considered:

- Buying a little smaller
- Looking a little further out
- Waiting another year to save more

We want you in a home you love—without hating the payment.

The Emotional Cost of Overextending

Here's the part no spreadsheet captures:
The emotional toll.

We've watched people who bought too much house:

- Stop investing in their marriage
- Stop spending time with friends
- Skip their kids' activities because they picked up more hours
- Feel anxious every time the car makes a noise

Homeownership is supposed to create security. A nest. A base for your life.

When it's done wrong, it does the opposite.

We're not telling you this to judge you.
We're telling you because we've seen it happen.
We've lived it.

We've bought too much house ourselves.
We've eaten ramen for months, trying to float two mortgages.
We've looked at our spouse across the dinner table and wondered if we were idiots.

We learned.
We changed.
Now we teach.

Because no one else was honest with us at the time.

Let's Talk About Cars and Lifestyle Debt

Here's another trap that quietly kills budgets: car payments.

We've met buyers who have two $800 car payments. That's $1,600 a month before you even talk about housing.

Add in insurance and gas—now it's over $2,000 easy.

Then they come to us and say:
"We want to buy a $500,000 house."

But their car habits say otherwise.

It's not that we think you shouldn't have a nice car. We just want you to see the whole picture.

Some lenders will qualify you based on gross income and current debts. If you're spending 20% of your take-home on cars, that's less room for housing—and less flexibility for everything else.

We always ask:

"If you had to choose, would you rather have the fancy car or the safer mortgage?"

You get to choose.
Just know the cost of your choice.

The Cost of "Just Because You Can"

Let's also talk about the phrase:

"But they said we're approved for it!"

We've heard it a thousand times.

Yes, you're approved.
Because they can sell the loan.
Because it fits the guidelines.
Because it closes the deal.

Approval is a **technical yes**.
It's not a personal recommendation.

It doesn't mean it's good for you.

We tell clients all the time:
"Just because you can doesn't mean you should."

You can eat fast food every day.
You can max out your credit cards.
You can buy the biggest house on the block.

Doesn't mean you'll love living with it.

Planning for Maintenance, Taxes, and Insurance

We see buyers who only think about **principal and interest**.

But owning a home includes:

- Property taxes (which go up over time)
- Homeowners insurance
- Mortgage insurance (if you're putting less than 20% down)
- HOA dues in many neighborhoods
- Ongoing maintenance

We coach buyers to think about the **total payment**.

We walk them through it.
We even encourage them to get insurance quotes early—so there are no surprises.

A $50/month difference in insurance is $600/year.
That adds up—especially when you're already stretching.

Questions We Ask Every Buyer

Here's what we want every client to answer before shopping:

- What is your current rent or housing payment?
- How does it feel right now? Tight? Comfortable?
- How much are you saving monthly?
- Do you have an emergency fund?
- What do you spend on dining, subscriptions, travel?
- What would you be willing to give up for a higher payment?
- What wouldn't you be willing to give up?
- How stable is your income?

We don't ask to be nosy.
We ask because these answers **matter**.

Reality Budget vs. Fantasy Budget

You need to understand the difference between the budget you **hope** you'll live on and the one you actually do.

The fantasy budget says:

- "We'll stop eating out."
- "We'll cancel streaming."
- "We'll cook every night."
- "We'll cut back on coffee."

Sounds noble.

But we're human.
We get tired.
We want comfort.
We celebrate.
We break routines.

That's not failure.
That's life.

So we tell our clients:

"Plan for who you really are. Not who you hope to be under pressure."

A mortgage shouldn't require you to become someone else.
It should fit who you are right now.

Stories from Clients Who Did It Right

We love telling these stories.

One couple qualified for $4,800/month.
They chose a home with a $3,200/month payment.

"We want to travel. We want daycare. We want to save," they said.

They're the ones who send us referrals.
They're the ones who send Christmas cards with photos in front of their house.

They didn't sacrifice their life to own a home.
They made the home **fit** their life.

Another client was a single dad.

He qualified for more but said, "I want breathing room."

He bought a home $100,000 under his approval limit.

Three years later, he refinanced to drop PMI and had plenty of equity.

He told us, "Thanks for not pushing me."

We don't share these to brag.
We share them because they're **proof that this works**.

The Emotional Win

Imagine this for a moment:

Owning a home that **feels right**.
Payments that don't keep you up worrying.
Still having a budget for birthdays, holidays, and vacations.
The pride of knowing you made a smart choice.
No buyer's remorse.
No desperate budgeting.
No stress about the next paycheck.
No arguments about money.

That's the real win.
That's the goal.

Action Checklist: Define Your Comfort Zone

We won't leave you hanging.
Here's your real-world homework:

1. Know your rent payment. How does it feel now?
2. Track 60–90 days of spending. See where the money goes.
3. Test the new payment. Set aside the extra you'd spend on a mortgage—now.
4. Plan for taxes, insurance, and maintenance. Don't ignore the full cost.
5. Consider lifestyle goals. Travel? Hobbies? Kids' activities?
6. Check emergency savings. Have at least 3–6 months.
7. Talk with your loan officer honestly. Don't just ask what you qualify for—ask what you can live with.
8. Discuss with your partner. Align on the payment before you shop.

This is Mortgage Club.
We don't sugarcoat it.
We want you to be prepared.

Closing Pep Talk

You don't win Mortgage Club by buying the biggest house you can.
You win by buying the **right** house.

The one you can afford comfortably.
The one that doesn't chain you to your job or your debts.
The one that lets you sleep at night.

Your lender might approve you for more.
Your realtor might show you more.
Your friends might cheer you on to spend more.

But at the end of the day, **you're the one making the payment.**

Decide on your budget. Not theirs.

Welcome to Mortgage Club.

RULE #4:

Pick Your Weapon: Loan Types Decoded.

Mortgage Club Confession: The Loan You Pick . . . or the Loan Picked for You

By Rich Hanlin

Welcome back. Here we are at Rule Number Four. Pick your weapon. Don't let them pick it for you.

Let me say that again—because this rule gets broken more than any other: Choose your loan type. Don't let them pick it for you.

I'm going to tell you something I wish weren't true. After nearly 36 years in this industry, I've seen it over and over again: Loans aren't always chosen based on what's best for the buyer. They're often chosen based on what's best for the loan officer or the company. And that should concern you.

Some loan officers flat out say it: "If I can't make the maximum commission on this deal, I won't do it." Others are working out of their garage and are willing to take pennies just to keep the lights on. The problem is what happens in between those two extremes—because that's where most loan decisions are made. And borrowers are rarely told the truth.

When I started, there were over 400,000 licensed loan originators nationwide. As I sit here today, writing this in August 2025, that number has dropped below 90,000. Do you know what that means? Less competition. Fewer options. More control in the hands of fewer lenders. And more borrowers are getting shoved into loan types that benefit the lender, not the borrower.

Now, I'm not here to paint myself as a saint. I know what my time is worth. I know that some loans pay more than others. But if you're sitting across the desk from me, or on the other end of the phone, my job is to give you every option you qualify for—not just the ones that make me more money.

• • • • • • • • • • • • • • •

Let me give you a real example. A borrower qualifies for:

- 3% down Conventional
- 3.5% down FHA
- 100% USDA
- 0% down VA

You might assume they're all about the same. They're not.

Each of those loans has a completely different interest rate. Each one has a different monthly payment. Each one lands in a different place on the servicing market. And each one has completely different rules for mortgage insurance.

Let's break it down. VA loans come with a hefty upfront funding fee but no monthly mortgage insurance. USDA loans have a lower upfront fee, but do include a monthly mortgage insurance payment. FHA loans have both an upfront mortgage insurance premium and a monthly MI payment, which sticks around for the life of the loan unless you refinance. Conventional loans? No upfront fees, but you'll have monthly PMI unless you put 20% down—or pay to remove it later.

And every one of these options affects your payment, your closing costs, your total out-of-pocket, and your long-term equity position.

So let me ask you this: If your lender isn't showing you all the options, are they working for you—or are they working for themselves?

A true professional will not only show you all the loan types you qualify for . . . They'll also show you the internal options within the loan type.

You're quoted a 30-year fixed conventional loan? Great. But what's the cost if you buy the rate down? What happens if you go slightly higher and take a lender credit? What's the payment difference? What's the cost difference? What's the breakeven point?

These aren't just numbers—they're decisions that could save you tens of thousands of dollars. The problem is, most buyers never even hear these questions. And that's how people get trapped in the wrong loan.

If your loan officer isn't having these kinds of conversations with you . . .

If they're just handing you a loan scenario and saying "sign here" . . .

If your options aren't being laid out clearly and explained just like you're reading this right now?

Then you're probably being sold a loan. Not choosing one. And you're definitely not getting the best deal.

I've seen it too many times. It's why this chapter matters so much. You have to ask. You have to compare. You have to make sure the loan fits you—not them.

Because when the dust settles, you're the one making the payments. Not them. Not the company. Not the realtor. You.

Choose your loan type. Don't let them pick it for you.

The Two-Pill Choice

If someone handed you two pills—one heals, one kills—and told you to pick blindly, would you gamble?

Of course not.

So why let a lender choose your loan?

Let's get brutally honest. Most loan officers aren't financial advisors. They're commission-driven salespeople working within institutions that pay more for pushing certain loan types—especially the ones that hurt you long-term. They aren't all bad people, but their incentives are often misaligned with your best interests.

So here's the deal: You either control the loan—or the loan controls you. And if someone else is choosing your loan for you, you're not the buyer. You're the product.

This chapter is about taking your power back.

Fixed vs. ARM vs. Buydown vs. B.S.

There are three major loan types every buyer needs to understand:

- Fixed-Rate Mortgages
- Adjustable-Rate Mortgages (ARMs)
- Temporary Buydowns

And then . . . there's the glittery pile of creatively labeled nonsense—"exclusive buyer programs," "smart-start loans," "flex ARMs"—that often end in regret.

Let's dig into the real stuff.

Fixed-Rate Mortgages: The Unsexy Champion

A fixed-rate mortgage is like a paid-off Toyota—reliable, predictable, not flashy, and built to last.

Your interest rate stays the same for the life of the loan. No sudden jumps. No sneaky recalculations. Just steady payments for 15, 20, or 30 years.

When Fixed Makes Sense:

- You plan to stay 5+ years
- You want long-term budget stability
- Your income is reliable

Why Lenders Undersell Fixed Loans:
They make less. Period. Commissions are lower, there's no future rate adjustment to profit from, and there are no back-end surprises to convert into cash later.

But here's a little-known truth: Over 90% of financially secure buyers in 2024 locked into fixed rates. That's not a coincidence. That's survival instinct.

We love fixed-rate loans. They're the boring champions. And when the market gets messy, it's the boring loans that save people's sanity.

ARM Loans: The Shiny Object That Bites

Adjustable-rate mortgages (ARMs) start with a low teaser rate. For the first few years—3, 5, or 7—they seem like a dream.

Then the clock runs out.

The interest rate resets. Payments jump. Stress kicks in.

ARM Risks Clearly Explained:

- Payments can increase by $500–$1,500 overnight
- 40% of 2024 foreclosures were ARM-related
- Most borrowers never understood what they signed

Lenders love ARMs. They get paid more. They build rate adjustments into their future revenue. But you? You're gambling with your roof over your head.

Unless you have a firm exit plan or serious financial flexibility, ARMs are like juggling knives—blindfolded.

Temporary Rate Buydowns: Secret Weapon (When Used Right)

Buydowns reduce your interest rate temporarily—often for 1 to 3 years. The most common is a 2/1 Buydown, where your rate is 2% lower in year one and 1% lower in year two.

Here's the beauty: If the seller pays for it, it's essentially a gift.

When It's Smart:

- You expect to refinance in 1–3 years
- You're buying in a market where sellers are offering concessions

- You want lower payments now while easing into the full mortgage

Game-Changing Bonus:
If you refinance early, the leftover buydown money in the escrow account comes back to you—either toward your payoff or refunded. We've seen clients get $2,000–$5,000 back.

Buydowns aren't a gimmick when structured correctly. They're a short-term buffer in a long-term game.

Special Loans = Special Problems

"Exclusive VIP Rate Program."
"Private Client Advantage ARM."
"FlexCap 3/1."

If you hear these phrases, clutch your wallet.

These programs often include:

- Hidden resets
- Prepayment penalties
- Surprise fees
- Shifting amortization terms

Mortgage Club rule: If it sounds too customized to explain in plain English . . . it's probably too risky to sign.

"If you don't pick your loan,
your lender picks your future."
That's not a punchline. That's a warning.

Hot Loans in 2025 (And Why to Be Cautious)

1. **Hybrid ARM Loans** – They look fixed. But after the term of 3, 5, 7, or 10 years, they adjust—and bite.
2. **1% Down Programs** – Great headline. But the fine print disqualifies most buyers—and those who qualify often get hammered by PMI.
3. **USDA Zero-Down** – Amazing if your home is in a qualifying rural zone. But many don't find out until it's too late that they're just a block outside the boundary.

Lender Incentive Breakdown (The Math That Matters)

Here's how lender compensation really works behind the scenes:

Loan Type	Lender Commission Range
Fixed-Rate Loan	$1,200 – $2,000
ARM Loan	$3,000 – $5,500
Buydown (w/ rebate)	Additional 2–4% bonus
"Custom Program"	Whatever they can sell

One lender at a conference said,
"Switching a borrower from fixed to ARM is worth a vacation. Literally."

Now you know.

Real Borrower Stories (Beyond Greg)

Madison & Tyler – The 1% Down Disaster
They were excited first-time buyers. Good credit. Dual income. They were told the 1% down program was "perfect for their situation." Everything looked great—until underwriting. A last-minute discovery revealed their income exceeded the program's cap . . . by $73. They lost the house. Lost their earnest money. And worst of all—lost their trust in the process.

Rob – The Strategic Buydown
Rob used a seller-paid 2/1 buydown to reduce his first-year mortgage payment by $550/month. Those savings gave him breathing room during a job transition. When rates dropped sooner than expected, he refinanced in year two and received $3,200 back from the unused buydown escrow fund—money he immediately applied to reduce his principal. Strategic. Smooth. Zero regrets.

Jasmine – The "Fixed" That Wasn't
Jasmine thought she had a fixed loan. Her lender called it a "5-year fixed hybrid." She didn't realize it was an ARM in disguise. In year six, her payment jumped from $2,150 to

$3,500 almost overnight. She couldn't refinance because her home value had dropped. With no wiggle room, she defaulted in month 79.

The Red Flags Checklist

Here's what to watch for when discussing your loan:

- You're only shown one option
- They don't explain points or lender credits
- You don't understand your PMI terms
- They talk about rates, but never the monthly payment
- You feel rushed, confused, or pressured
- You hear "this program is exclusive"
- They never ask how long you'll live in the home

If more than one of these pops up, pause everything. You're being sold.

The Decision Matrix: Your Power Tool

Before you choose a loan, ask these five questions:

1. **What will be my starting rate, and what's the highest it could ever go?**
2. **What's the monthly payment from the start of the loan and in five years?**

3. **What's the total cost (including PMI, fees, etc.) over the first 5 years?**
4. **What happens if I refinance or sell in 2–3 years?**
5. **What does my loan officer make from this transaction?**

You deserve honest answers. If you don't get them, you don't sign.

Closing Pep Talk

Every buyer has the right to choose their loan. But most never realize it—because nobody tells them they're allowed to ask.

If you remember nothing else from this chapter, remember this:

The loan you choose is one of the most powerful decisions you'll make in your adult life.

It determines your payments. Your cash flow. Your peace of mind. Your ability to refinance, invest, or sell.

Pick wrong, and you might be stuck for years—paying more than you need to, with no easy way out.

Pick right, and you walk into your new home not just proud—but empowered.

So slow down. Ask more questions. And never let anyone rush you through one of the biggest decisions of your life.

Choose your loan type. Don't let them pick it for you.

This is Mortgage Club.
And now, you know this rule.

RULE #5:

Shop for a Rate Without Getting Shot.

Mortgage Club Confession: *The 5.25% Panic*

by Tim Rhey

They walked into my office like they'd just seen a ghost. A married couple in their 30s—smart, responsible, good income, first-time buyers—and completely panicked.

The husband was gripping a Loan Estimate like it was a live grenade.

"This other lender just quoted us 5.25% on a 30-year fixed," he said nervously. "It's way lower than what we've seen anywhere else. Are we being played . . . or should we just take it?"

At the time, 5.25% was considered a killer deal. My first instinct wasn't to match it—it was to challenge it.

"That's a strong rate," I said. "But be very careful—that rate may come at a cost."

They both blinked like I'd just spoken in code.

"What do you mean by cost? I thought all lenders basically charge the same fees."

And that, right there, is the myth that traps thousands of borrowers every year.

"Nope," I said. "Rates are only half the story. The other half? Cost. How much are you paying to get that rate?"

So we compared.

We sat down with their Loan Estimate and ran a side-by-side breakdown. Their offer had a gorgeous 5.25% headline rate, sure. But buried underneath? A whopping $18,000 in upfront fees—most of it disguised as "Discount Points."

By comparison, our rate was 5.5%, but our total costs were less than half.

"You're paying more up front for a slightly lower rate," I told them. "Over the next five years, you're actually losing money."

They were stunned. And grateful. And a little embarrassed.

"We almost signed this. We thought we were being smart."

They were smart. But they were also being baited by the oldest trick in the book: a low rate hiding a high cost.

• • • • • • • • • • • • • • •

Mortgage Club Confession Takeaway

The lowest rate doesn't always win.
If the cost to get that rate is sky-high, you're not saving—you're just spending in disguise.
Always compare the rate **and** cost side by side.
And if it seems too good to be true?
Trust your gut . . . then check the fine print.

Shop Smart Or Pay Dearly

Here's the ugly truth most borrowers don't know: 86% of buyers use the loan officer recommended by their real estate agent. Even fewer shop more than once. And almost no one compares all-in costs.

Worse? Most people think pulling your credit more than once will tank your score. So they pick one lender, take one quote, and close their eyes.

Let's clear this up. Let's get smart. Because shopping like a pro isn't just savvy—it's survival.

Debunking The Credit Pull Myth

Let's say this first, loud and clear:

Mortgage credit pulls don't work like credit card pulls.

FICO understands that smart buyers shop for loans. That's why mortgage-related credit inquiries made within a 30-day window are treated as a **single** inquiry for scoring purposes.

You could pull your credit with three different mortgage lenders in one week, and your score would likely drop zero to five points. That's it.

Not 30. Not 50. Not the "kiss of death" you've heard online.

But here's the trick: **You can't mix credit pulls.** If you pull with a mortgage lender, then a car dealer, then a furniture store . . . now your score gets bruised.

So shop smartly—but don't be scared.
Fear favors the lender. Knowledge favors you.

"I Trusted Them" Shouldn't Be Your Strategy

Most buyers go with the person their agent recommends.

Should you get a quote from that person? Sure. But should you stop there? Absolutely not.

Here's why: Your agent may do one or two deals a year. Their preferred lender may only close a few loans per month. Compare that to a broker who closes 15–30 files monthly across multiple agents, programs, and platforms.

Experience matters. Volume matters. Transparency matters more.

You wouldn't walk into a dealership, ask for a car, and take the first one they hand you.

Yet, when it comes to mortgages—arguably the biggest financial decision of your life—people hand over their credit, income, future, and peace of mind to the first person who answers the phone.

Time to flip the script.

Why this Chapter Matters

This chapter will show you:

- How to get quotes without damaging your credit
- What to ask for (and what to avoid)
- Why fees matter more than rates
- How we shop for our own family
- Real examples of bait-and-switch tactics
- Your ultimate Rate Shopping Checklist

We're not anti-lender. We are **anti-blind-trust**. We're **pro-transparency**. Pro-confidence. Pro-strategy.

Because when you shop smart, you win.

When you don't?

Well . . . just rewind to the couple who paid $18,000 for the "best rate" in town.

Most people "shop" by calling three lenders and asking one question:

"What's your rate?"

That's like asking a car dealership, "How much for a car?" without telling them the make, model, year, color, or options.

Let's get clear: A **mortgage rate quote means nothing** unless it includes the following:

1. **The interest rate**
2. **The APR**
3. **The lender fees**
4. **The loan program type**
5. **The lock period**
6. **The points or credits involved**
7. **The estimated closing costs and monthly payment**
8. **Whether the quote is locked or floating**

Miss one of these? You're comparing apples to aardvarks.

The Quote Script That Works

Here's how to shop like a pro:

You: "Hi, I'm shopping for a mortgage and looking for transparency. I'll be asking each lender for a full quote that includes the rate, APR, closing costs, points or credits, and whether the rate is locked. Can you provide that?"

If they say yes? Great. Proceed.

If they hedge, deflect, or say they need to pull credit first? Red flag.

Don't Just Chase The Lowest Rate

The lowest rate doesn't always mean the best deal.

If one lender quotes 5.625% and another quotes 5.75%, you might be tempted to go with the lower rate—until you find out they're charging **$9,000 in discount points** to buy it down.

What matters is the **total cost over time**, not just the shiny number up front.

Ask for a **side-by-side comparison** of:

- Payment over 5 years
- Closing costs
- Breakeven point
- Total interest paid

You may find that a slightly higher rate with a lender credit actually saves you more in year one—or gives you extra cash to pay down other debt.

We don't just talk this stuff—we live it.

We've worked with clients who brought us quotes from banks, builders, retail lenders, and online shops. And nine times out of ten, when we peeled back the layers, there was a better deal hiding in plain sight.

Sometimes it wasn't a better rate. It was **fewer fees**. Or **greater flexibility**. Or **faster turnaround times**. Or **better advice** that saved them thousands later.

We don't promise the lowest rate in the universe.

We promise to help you understand the numbers, choose what fits your goals, and **never get played.**

That's Mortgage Club.

Making Sense of the Rate Lock

Let's tackle one of the most misunderstood concepts in mortgage shopping: **the rate lock.**

You don't get the rate a lender *tells* you.
You get the rate a lender *locks* for you.

And here's the kicker: most quotes aren't locked.

"What's Your Rate?"— The Lender's Favorite Trick

Lenders love to quote floating rates—rates that *could* be locked but aren't.
Why? Because they can always say, "Well, that rate was available when we talked. Now it's gone."

It gives them wiggle room. Leverage. Power.

If they quote you a killer rate to win your business, but then the market shifts or they never lock it, you're stuck.

And by the time you find out, you're already deep in underwriting and emotionally invested in the home.

That's not a quote. That's a bait-and-switch.

How Rate Locks Actually Work

- **Lock periods** usually come in 15, 30, 45, and 60-day options.
- The longer the lock, the more expensive the rate.
- Rates can typically only be locked **once your application is complete**—and sometimes only after credit is pulled and disclosures are signed.
- Once locked, that rate holds unless the lock expires, your loan changes, or you switch properties.

So when someone says, "Yeah, we can do 5.75%," your next question should always be:

"Great—can you lock it right now, and will you send me the lock confirmation in writing?"

If they pause. Dodge. Say, "Let's wait until later."

That's your cue. Walk.

The Rebate Game

Let's talk **lender credits**—aka rebates.

Sometimes, taking a slightly higher rate allows the lender to give you a credit at closing, which can cover:

- Title fees
- Appraisal fees
- Escrow deposits
- Underwriting fees
- Buydowns

This is how strategic buyers stack savings—especially when pairing lender credits with seller concessions.

But not all lenders offer rebates the same way. Some pocket the profit instead of passing it on to you. Others structure it with vague math and hidden markups.

A true Mortgage Club lender will show you **the raw pricing**, explain the trade-offs, and build a scenario that fits your cash flow goals—not theirs.

The Truth About Rate Sheets

Here's something most lenders won't admit: **Every lender has access to the same bond market.**

That means rates across lenders should be very similar—if you're comparing apples to apples.

So, when someone quotes you a rate that's **a half-point lower** than everyone else?

Be skeptical.

That often means:

- Hidden fees
- Temporary teaser rates
- Inflated title or escrow charges
- Misleading assumptions about credit, property type, or down payment

If a quote sounds too good to be true, it probably is.

Ask for the Loan Estimate (LE).
Ask for the APR.
Ask for the math.

Because in this business, **the truth is always in the details**.

By now, you know the truth: not all quotes are real, not all lenders are transparent, and shopping smart takes more than filling out a few online forms.

So what does a Mortgage Club-level shopper actually do?

You follow this **Mortgage Club Rate Shopper Blueprint**.

Step 1: Start With Strategy, Not Rate

Before you chase the lowest number, answer these questions:

- What's your budget comfort zone?
- How long do you plan to live in the home?
- How much money do you want to keep in your pocket after closing?
- Do you plan to refinance if rates drop?
- Are you using seller concessions?

These answers shape your rate target, your cost structure, and your loan program. Without this clarity, you're just rate-chasing in the dark.

Step 2: Know Your Credit And Cash Flow Position

You should walk into every lender conversation knowing:

- Your exact credit score from all three bureaus
- Your monthly debts and obligations
- Your target down payment

- Your reserve funds
- Your monthly income (gross and net)

This is your ammo. It prevents lenders from assuming, guessing, or misclassifying your file, which often leads to a higher rate.

Pro tip: Get your **full tri-merge credit report** from one source, and use it with every lender. It eliminates confusion and keeps you in control.

Step 3: Ask For Options—Then Demand The Truth

You want **three clear comparisons**:

1. **Base rate scenario**: lowest cost, par rate
2. **Buydown option**: lower rate, higher cost
3. **Lender credit option**: higher rate, lower cost

Each should include:

- Interest rate
- Monthly payment
- Total cash to close
- Loan Estimate (LE)
- APR

If they won't send it in writing, they don't deserve your business.

Step 4: Keep A Tracking Sheet

Create a simple chart with these columns:

Lender | Rate | Points | Fees | Credits | Payment | Lock Term | APR |

We've seen clients get quoted five different "lowest rates" in 24 hours.

Without a tracking sheet, it's impossible to compare.

Step 5: Lock Strategically—Not Emotionally

Here's what we tell every client:

"If the rate fits your budget, your plan, and your long-term goals, and you're under contract—lock it."

The perfect rate doesn't exist.

You're not chasing perfection. You're chasing alignment.

And the real win is closing confidently—not getting ghosted at the finish line because your lender never locked.

The Mindset Reset: Don't Flinch

By now, you've learned how to shop smart. But shopping is only half the battle.

You have to stay calm, clear, and **confident** throughout the entire process—because this is where most buyers panic and give up. They start strong . . . and then fold when the paperwork piles up, when rates move, or when their buddy tells them they "could've gotten a lower rate."

When you shop multiple lenders, they will **sense your confidence**—or your fear.

You must control the tone. That means:

- Asking direct questions
- Requesting written proof
- Not apologizing for shopping around
- Not being baited by "act now" pressure

You're not a tire-kicker. You're a high-stakes buyer making a six-figure decision. Act like it.

Remember Who Works For Who

We say it over and over, and it's worth saying again:

The lender works for you.
Not the other way around.

If your questions annoy them, you've just dodged a bullet. If they hesitate to give you a comparison, you've caught them. If they try to guilt you into loyalty—congratulations, you just exposed their game.

Good lenders *love* educated borrowers. They want you to compare. They're not afraid of competition—because they know they're bringing value.

Final Buyer Script: Power In Your Pocket

Here's what to say when you're close to choosing a lender:

"I've received quotes from three lenders. I'm looking at the rate, fees, and total cost of the loan. I'm not just chasing the lowest rate—I'm choosing based on transparency, trust, and long-term fit. Can you show me how your offer compares?"

Mic drop.

This statement disarms weak lenders and attracts the right ones. It shows you're serious. Strategic. Educated. Mortgage Club material.

Close With Conviction

Once you've gathered the data...
Once you've reviewed the options...
Once you've locked the loan that fits your plan—

Stop shopping.

Don't second-guess. Don't torture yourself. Don't scroll forums looking for people who "got a better deal."

Trust your prep. Trust your plan. Trust your instincts.

Because here's what really separates Mortgage Club graduates from the rest:

We don't just shop smarter—we close stronger.

Welcome to Mortgage Club.

RULE #6:

Points, Fees, and Mortgage Math Games

Mortgage Club Confession

From Rich Hanlin

Let me say this again, louder for the people in the back: **Understand your points, fees, and buydowns.**

This is the landmine zone. And for many borrowers, it's where the damage happens.

Let's talk about John.

John came in demanding the lowest rate available. Like a lot of people, he'd read some headline or talked to a buddy at the gym and now thought the magic number was everything. So we pulled up that day's rate sheet—which most people don't even realize exists. On any given day, there's a range. A big one. Maybe as low as 2%, maybe as high as 10%.

But what do people usually see?

"Today's rate is 6.75% with no points."
Or
"6.5% with one point."

That's the marketing. That's the internet. And that's the start of a dangerous game if you don't understand what you're buying.

John? He wanted 2%. No matter the cost. And when I say no matter the cost, I mean it. It would've taken over **$85,000 in discount points**—just to buy the rate down that low. That's not counting lender fees. Not counting title. Not counting my compensation.

And here's the kicker…

The amount John would've saved by getting that lower rate? **Less than the cost of buying it.**

He would've lost money trying to save money.

How sad is that?

Now, here's where it gets spicier. Turns out, John had an ulterior motive. He was headed for a divorce. He didn't want to tell us, but we figured it out through the red flags:

- He was unusually pushy about the payment.
- He didn't care about the long-term math.
- He was willing to use the equity in the house—without his wife's knowledge—to improve his financial position.

One small problem:
California is a community property state.
Fifty percent of that equity? It wasn't his. It was hers.

So why try to lock in a low rate at all costs?

Because John wanted to stay in the home, pay her out, and lower his expenses—without full disclosure. He was using mortgage strategy to try to tilt the balance of a pending divorce settlement.

Dangerous. Legally and financially.

In the end, we walked John through a real cost-benefit conversation. The result?

He didn't buy down the rate.
He didn't waste $85,000.
And the deal didn't become a legal disaster.

• • • • • • • • • • • • • • •

The truth is:

Every fee, every point, every buydown needs to pass two tests.

1. **Does it align with your real goals?**
2. **Does it make mathematical sense in your timeline?**

Because here's the reality of the mortgage world:
Nothing is free.
Some things are outrageously expensive.
And most people selling you something have a personal pocketbook bias.

So, if you're going to do this right?

Find someone who'll shoot you straight.
Ask what the breakeven point really is.

And don't let the dream of a lower rate cloud your judgment.

Because one wrong move with points and fees?
It could cost you more than just money.

It could cost you trust, equity, and even your future stability.

That's the real confession.

The Truth About Points, Fees, and Buydowns

If you're reading this, you're about to learn the real game behind "today's rates" and why that 6.125% APR you saw on Zillow is about as real as a Hollywood hairline.

The world of **points, lender fees, and rate buydowns** is where sneaky lenders eat their lunch. It's where the numbers get fuzzy, the language gets technical, and otherwise smart buyers nod politely—while quietly getting fleeced.

But **not you.**
Not this time.

Let's go.

First: What Are Points?

Points are fees you can pay upfront to **buy down your interest rate.**
One point = 1% of your loan amount.

So on a $400,000 loan, one point = $4,000.

Lenders will often show you something like:

- 6.875% (no points)
- 6.625% (pay 1 point)
- 6.5% (pay 1.5 points)

Looks like a simple trade, right?
Lower rate = pay a little more upfront.

But the **math behind that trade** is everything.

If the monthly savings from that lower rate takes **7 years to break even**, and you're only planning to stay in the house for 4 years?

You just paid to save someone else money.

The lender wins.
The seller wins.
Even the next buyer might win.

But you?
You just lit money on fire.

The Buydown Illusion

Here's the dirty little secret:
Most lenders **love** selling rate buydowns.

Why?

Because it **inflates their margins.**
Because it sounds sexy.
And because it makes you feel like you're getting a deal—even when you're not.

There are two types of buydowns we see most often:

1. **Permanent Buydown** – You pay points to permanently reduce your rate.
2. **Temporary Buydown** – You (or the seller) pay to lower the rate temporarily (e.g., 2-1 buydown).

Let's talk temporary buydowns real quick...

They can be legit.
If the **seller is paying for it**, and it buys you breathing room in the first 1–2 years of payments while your income grows or you plan a refinance, awesome.

But if **you're the one paying**, and it doesn't reduce your rate long-term?

You're just prepaying your own loan with a fancy label on it.

Let's Talk Fees

Now we're stepping into the casino.

Because closing costs are where lenders, brokers, and shady shops **really** make their money—especially if you don't know what to look for.

Common fees:

- **Origination fee** – Sometimes legit. Sometimes junk. Ask questions.
- **Underwriting fee** – Charged by the lender for reviewing your file. Reasonable if under $1,200.
- **Processing fee** – Sometimes bundled with underwriting. Sometimes extra fluff.
- **Discount points** – This is your buydown cost.
- **Appraisal, credit, title, escrow** – Standard and usually can't be negotiated.

What you're looking for is anything labeled as **"lender fee"** or **"broker fee"** with a big round number attached to it.

If they're charging you $2,995 and you don't know why? **Red flag.**

If they can't explain exactly what you're paying—and why it benefits you?
Red flag.

If they're quoting you a smoking hot rate that "only costs two points" but won't show you the breakeven timeline? **Fire alarm.**

Be the Buyer Who Asks the Question

We've said it before, and we'll say it again:
You don't need to be a mortgage expert. But you can take the lessons of the Mortgage Club and apply them to be strategic.

Ask:

- "What's the breakeven point on this buydown?"
- "What would the payment be if I didn't pay points?"
- "Can you show me a zero-point option side-by-side?"
- "What are all the lender-specific fees on this loan?"

And if the answers don't feel honest?
Run.

You've got options.
You've got leverage.
And if you're reading this book, you've got us in your corner.

Smart Math vs. Smooth Talk

How to Spot a Bad Deal Before You Sign It

Let's set the scene.

You're sitting across from a smiling lender. They've got shiny graphs, slick software, and a buttoned-up blazer that says, "Trust me, I'm a professional."

They quote you a rate.

They show you a beautiful monthly payment.

Then they pause and smile. Like they just handed you the keys to the kingdom.

But here's the truth: **Numbers lie—when you don't ask the right questions.**

Let's break this down.

Example:

Scenario A:
6.5% interest rate
No points
$3,100 monthly payment

Scenario B:
6.25% interest rate
Costs 2 points (about $8,000)
$3,000 monthly payment

Looks like Scenario B saves you $100/month. Sweet deal, right?

But if it takes **80 months** to make up that $8,000?

That's **6.6 years** just to break even.

What if you sell in 5?
Refi in 3?
Change jobs and move in 2?

You **lose** money.

So, unless you're planning to stay long-term and have that extra cash to spare, the "better rate" might actually be the **worst move.**

The Breakeven Point: Your New Best Friend

Here's the golden question to ask your lender every time they try to sell you a buydown or points:

"What's the breakeven point?"

If they can't answer it?
They're not doing math—they're doing **sales.**

The breakeven point tells you exactly how many months it will take for the money you spent upfront to start saving you money.

If you plan to stay in the home **longer than the breakeven point**, it might be a good idea.

Shorter than that?
Don't even think about it.

Real Buyer, Real Regret

We had a client once—let's call her Stephanie.

Stephanie was sharp, successful, and came in with a printout from a competitor showing a 5.875% rate.

"I want to match this," she said.

We ran the numbers. That rate required her to pay **three points**—over **$21,000** on her $700,000 loan.

Breakeven point on that loan? **9 years**.

Stephanie planned to sell in **4 years**.

When we showed her the math, she almost dropped her latte.

She ended up taking our zero-point rate at 6.5%, and while the payment was a little higher, she saved over $20K at closing—and still had the flexibility to move in 4 years without a loss.

Here's What a Good Lender Will Do

A good lender won't push one rate or product.
A good lender will:

- Show you **multiple scenarios**
- Walk through **breakeven math**
- Help you make the call based on your **goals**, not theirs
- Never pressure you into spending upfront money to "feel better" about the rate

And if they ever say, "Don't worry about the fees, just look at the payment"?
Worry. A lot.

The Red Flag Checklist: How to Smell a Bad Lender in Under 60 Seconds

There's something about the mortgage industry that attracts both legends and liars.
And when it comes to points, fees, and "rate specials," the smoke-and-mirrors game gets even trickier.

Here's your checklist.
If your lender does two or more of these, **run.**

Red Flag #1: "Let me just get you the lowest payment."
Translation: "I'm not going to show you the full cost breakdown, just a sexy number to get you excited."

Red Flag #2: "Don't worry about points—it's normal."
Wrong. There's nothing "normal" about spending thousands upfront unless it fits your long-term plan.

Red Flag #3: They won't give you a Loan Estimate.
If they say, "We'll give it to you later," or only email screenshots, they're hiding something.

Red Flag #4: "Trust me, this is what everyone does."
Everyone loses money if they follow the herd. You're not everyone.

Red Flag #5: You feel rushed.
Great lenders move fast **with** you, not **at** you. Pressure is a tactic, not a service.

What You Should Expect Instead

A lender who...

- **Explains every cost.**
  Not in industry jargon—but in plain language, you could explain to your grandma.
- **Shows you all your options.**
  Even the ones that don't pay them as much.
- **Calculates your breakeven** and helps you decide if the buydown is worth it.
- **Listens to your timeline, your goals, and your budget.**
  Because guess what? Your mortgage should work for you—not the other way around.

If It Feels Too Good to Be True...

It probably is.

We once had a client who said, "This other lender quoted me 5.25% with no points!"

We said, "That's a great rate. Send us the Loan Estimate."

What we saw?

- $6,000 in lender fees
- Inflated title and escrow costs
- A "discount" that wasn't a discount at all—just baked into the price

Total closing costs? Over $14,000 more than what we quoted at a slightly higher rate.

She almost signed it.
But after comparing apples to apples, she went with us – and saved thousands.

The Bottom Line

It's not just about the rate.
It's about the **real cost** of borrowing money.

And sometimes, the better deal is the one with the higher rate and lower upfront cost.

Because smart buyers know:
The best mortgage isn't the lowest rate—it's the one that fits your life.

Your Points & Fees Strategy Template (Because You're Not Just a Borrower—You're a Strategist)

Let's end this chapter the way all great fights end: with a winning strategy.

Below is the exact breakdown we walk through with every smart Mortgage Club borrower who wants to outplay the mortgage casino. Print it. Share it. Tattoo it if you must. This is how you avoid walking away with a financial black eye.

1. Know Your Timeline

Ask yourself:
How long am I going to keep this loan?
Not the house—the loan.

If you plan to refinance in a year or sell in two, paying $6,000 to buy down the rate doesn't make sense. Your breakeven point might be five years away, and you'll never recoup the cost.

Short-term = prioritize **low fees**
Long-term = evaluate **rate buydowns carefully**

2. Get the Real Numbers, Not the Marketing

Ask your lender for a **Loan Estimate (LE)** that includes:

- Rate
- Points (as a percentage AND dollar figure)
- Origination fees
- Third-party fees
- Total cash to close
- APR (not just the note rate)

A good lender will hand this over quickly. A shady one will dodge.
Never compare lenders without LEs side-by-side.

3. Calculate Your Breakeven Like a Pro

Here's how:

- Find the cost of the buydown (e.g., 1 point = $3,000)
- Divide that by the monthly savings from the lower rate
- That's how many months it takes to "break even"

Example:

- Cost = $3,000
- Monthly savings = $42
- Breakeven = 71 months (almost 6 years)

Will you keep the loan that long?
If not, don't buy it.

4. Challenge the "Best Rate" Pitch

A lower rate **might** not be the best option.

Ask:

- "What's the difference in payment vs. upfront cost?"
- "How much more am I spending to save $40 a month?"
- "Does this make sense for my situation?"

Remember: lenders get paid differently based on what you choose. Some may steer you toward the option that pays **them** more.

You're here to protect your money, not their commission.

5. Avoid Emotional Decisions

Desperation makes for bad math.

If you're scrambling to lower your payment at all costs, stop. Zoom out. Breathe. Let the numbers speak.

The best loan decisions are made with **data**, not fear.

6. Get a Second Opinion

If something feels off, it probably is.

Email the Loan Estimate to a trusted broker or mortgage expert. Ask them to decode it. A second set of eyes can save you thousands—and a future regret spiral.

"But I already signed disclosures!"
Doesn't matter. Until you close, you're not locked in.

Final Thought: Be the One Who Asks

Most borrowers don't ask.
They nod. They sign. They regret it later.

You're not most borrowers.

You're the one who asks:
"What's this fee for?"
"Is this worth it?"
"How does this impact my long-term plan?"

And because you ask, you win.

Because asking is the new negotiating.
And negotiating is how you own your outcome.

RULE #7:

Steal from the Seller (Legally).

Mortgage Club Confession: The $1M Mental Block

-By Tim Rhey

Not long ago, an older couple called my office to ask for some quick advice.

They had just found their dream home—a stunning Colorado mountain property—listed just over $1 million. It had everything: views, privacy, charm, and that timeless *this-is-where-we'll-die-happy* kind of energy.

But there was one problem.

"We really don't want to go over a million," they told me. "That's our line in the sand."

I asked the obvious question:

"Why?"

Without hesitation, the husband said:

"Because once you go over a million, the payment gets out of hand."

I nodded. It's a common mindset—especially for retirees or people buying what they believe will be their final home. But instead of just accepting the limit, I pulled out the numbers.

We compared two scenarios:

- One with a $1,000,000 purchase price.
- One with a $1,100,000 purchase price.

To their surprise, the payment difference wasn't that dramatic to them.

But then I showed them something else—something that shifted the whole conversation.

"What if . . . instead of pushing so hard on the list price, we asked the seller to pay to buy down your interest rate?"

Their eyes widened. The light bulb went on.

They had been laser-focused on purchase price—which is fine. But when it came down to it, what really mattered to them was the monthly payment.

And in this case, the right seller concession strategy meant they could afford the $1.1M home with a payment that was actually lower than the $1M option—all because the seller chipped in to buy down the rate.

Instead of squeezing the price down $50K—which many sellers resist—they submitted a full-price offer with a concession request to cover a rate buydown.

And it worked.

The seller agreed.

The couple locked in a low monthly payment.

And they moved into their mountain dream home with peace of mind.

• • • • • • • • • • • • • • •

Mortgage Club Reality:

You can't live in a purchase price—you live in a monthly payment.

If the goal is affordability, don't just negotiate price . . . negotiate structure.

A seller credit toward your rate can often do more for your monthly comfort than a price cut ever will.

The best deal isn't always the lowest price—it's the smartest structure.

That couple taught me something that day, too:

Sometimes, the biggest roadblock isn't the price—it's the way we think about the price.

They walked away not only with the house they wanted . . . but with a custom mortgage strategy that made it feel like they paid less—even when they technically didn't.

They accomplished their goals without giving up the dream view, the kitchen they loved, or the peace of knowing they played the game like a boss.

Secrets of Concessions

Let's get one thing straight: **concessions aren't handouts. They're tools.** Weapons, actually.

In a market where every dollar counts—and buyers are often cash poor—seller credits can make or break a deal.

But if you don't know how to ask, structure, or negotiate for them . . . they vanish.

Poof. Gone.

And you end up covering costs that someone else might've been happy to pay.

We've helped negotiate millions in seller credits—sometimes quietly, sometimes aggressively, and sometimes like magicians pulling money out of thin air.

The secret? Strategy, timing, and knowing the rules better than the other side.

The NAR Settlement Changed Everything

In 2024, the National Association of Realtors agreed to a seismic shift: sellers no longer had to pay the buyer's agent commission.

Sounds simple. But it flipped negotiations on their head.

Suddenly, buyers had to consider paying their own agent out of pocket—on top of down payments, closing costs, moving expenses, and all the unexpected life stuff that already comes with buying a home.

Here's the problem: most buyers can't afford that.

The average American has less than $500 in savings.

So if you're buying a home in this market, you're likely tight on funds—and you're not alone.

But the good news? There are still ways to win.

Concessions 101: What They Are and How They Work

Seller concessions are credits the seller agrees to give you at closing—typically to help cover closing costs or reduce your interest rate.

They're not illegal. They're not shady. In fact, they're fully baked into the rules of Fannie Mae, Freddie Mac, FHA, and VA guidelines.

Here's the golden formula:

- **Conventional loans (primary residence):** 3% to 9% max, depending on down payment
- **FHA:** Up to 6% seller concessions allowed
- **VA:** Up to 4%, plus additional credits in some cases

You just have to ask.

But most agents don't ask.

And most lenders don't suggest it—because it requires more work, more communication, and sometimes, slightly lower profits.

Too bad. We're not most.

"Negotiation isn't confrontation—it's collaboration with leverage."

Structure Wins Deals: How to Frame Offers That Get Seller Credits

You don't get what you don't ask for.

But just asking isn't enough.

You have to structure the offer the right way, or the seller—and their agent—will see it as sloppy, desperate, or offensive.

We've seen too many deals fall apart because buyers demanded a $50,000 discount and $20,000 in seller credits and a rate buydown, and asked the seller to cover the buyer's agent fee.

That's not negotiation. That's a tantrum wrapped in paperwork.

Let's get tactical.

If a home is listed at $350,000 and the seller is willing to take $340,000, we'll structure it like this:

- **Offer price**: $350,000
- **Seller concessions**: $10,000 toward closing costs
- **Net to seller**: $340,000

The seller gets what they want.

You get what you need.

Everybody wins.

That's the core of smart negotiating. But most people don't even know it's an option.

The "Raise and Credit" Strategy

Here's how we explain it to our buyers:

"If you were planning to offer $320,000 on that home—but you're short $10,000 in closing funds—we'll go in at $330,000, ask the seller to credit $10,000 back to you, and make sure the appraised value can support it. The seller still nets $320,000, and you don't drain your bank account to close. Sound good?"

We've used this play for first-time buyers, veterans, move-up buyers, and even seasoned investors who want to preserve capital.

It's clean. It's ethical. And it works—especially when the seller understands the end result.

Don't Rely on the Realtor Alone

This is where most deals die.

Buyers assume their agent is handling the strategy.

But the agent assumes the lender is handling the math.

And the lender assumes the buyer already knows their options.

See the problem?

You're the only one truly accountable for making sure the deal is structured in your best interest.

That doesn't mean you have to be a mortgage expert—that's our job.

But it does mean you should join the Mortgage Club to understand the basics and partner with a team that gives a damn enough to walk you through every option—even the complicated ones.

We've coached buyers through seller concessions that:

- Covered full agent commissions post-NAR settlement
- Paid for full 3-2-1 rate buydowns to lower payments starting in year one
- Eliminated all closing costs
- Covered debt payoff to help qualify
- Reduced PMI
- Even paid off solar panels and HOA transfer fees

It's not about getting greedy—it's about negotiating smart and protecting your future cash flow.

Seller Concession Strategy Template

If you want to make your offer pop while still protecting your wallet, here's a simple structure you can follow with your lender and agent:

1. **Decide Your Net Offer:** What amount do you want the seller to walk away with?
2. **Add Your Desired Credit:** Add the amount you'd like to receive toward closing costs or rate buydown.
3. **Confirm Appraisal Room:** Make sure the final offer price will still appraise.
4. **Submit With Clarity:** Explain the structure in your offer so it's easy for the seller to say yes.

Here's a sample format:

"Buyer is offering $500,000, which includes a $10,000 credit to be used toward closing costs and/or interest rate buydown. Seller net proceeds to remain at $490,000."

That sentence alone can save you thousands.

The 2025 Reality: Leverage Is Everything

Post-COVID and post-settlement, this market is not for the faint of heart.

You've got to come prepared, ask the right questions, and be bold in the right places.

The seller credit game isn't new—but the stakes are higher now than ever before.

With higher rates, tighter budgets, and more buyers leaning on concessions, it's become the sharpest tool in the offer-writing shed.

We're not saying every deal needs one.

But if you're not at least discussing it, you're likely leaving money on the table.

And for what? To avoid an awkward conversation?

No thanks.

We'll take the thousands in savings and let the other guys nod politely to their overpriced, under-leveraged deal.

The Closing Line

"You can't live in a price tag. You live in a payment."

Use your leverage.
Negotiate like a boss.
And never forget—sellers are often just as motivated as you are.
They want to close.
Help them help you.

Welcome to Mortgage Club.

RULE #8:

Get Your Paperwork Right. Or Get Wrecked.

Mortgage Club Confession: Paperwork Twins, Nightmare Journeys

-Rich Hanlin

This one always hits differently. There's no single borrower story for this rule—because this is the story of almost every loan.

You can have two borrowers with the exact same loan amount, the exact same credit score, the same monthly income, and on paper—identical profiles. But the journey to get that loan closed? Couldn't be more different.

Let's break it down.

One borrower walks in, salaried, and has been on the same job for ten years. That's what we call a "vanilla loan." It's the mortgage version of autopilot. No surprises. No weird income documentation. I could close that file in my sleep with a single pay stub and a W-2. Clean. Easy. Done.

Then there's the other guy.

Self-employed. Gaps in work history. Multiple job changes in the past two years. A mix of retirement income, freelance 1099 work, and a small business that technically runs out of his garage. Spouse has an unrelated income stream. No recent tax filing because they're on an extension.

They might still qualify for the same loan. The income calculation might be identical in the end. But the road to get there? One's a sidewalk, the other's a jungle trail.

That's the part most people don't understand.

And this is why working with a pro matters. A real pro doesn't just dump a checklist in your lap and ask for everything under the sun. We look at your profile and say, "Okay, based on your situation, here's what we're really going to need. And here's where we might hit a bump."

For borrower one? We say, "Hang on to your most recent pay stub. We're good until go-time."

For borrower two? Whole different conversation.

We're checking what year they last filed taxes. If it's the most recent last two years, great. We'll average those two years of income. But now we're looking deeper. Can we add back depreciation? Was there a dip in income year over year? Was that because of COVID or some other disruption?

We're not just collecting paper—we're decoding the entire story of your income.

And sometimes, the story reads like a thriller.

• • • • • • • • • • • • • • • •

Look, not every lender is the same. Some have overlays—extra paperwork requirements, just because. But that's not standard. The real key is matching your loan to the right lender *and* prepping your paperwork like it's going in front of a federal judge.

Because it might as well be.

Your job is to be honest. Our job is to be prepared. Together, we create a roadmap to approval that doesn't crash at the finish line.

That's what we mean by dialing it in. No surprises. No panic. Just a smooth, smart, locked-in path to the keys.

Underwriting: Not A Mystical Force, Just A Mathematical Machine

Let's demystify underwriting right now. It's not a wizard in a dark room with a crystal ball. It's a **matrix** of risk guidelines built by Fannie Mae, Freddie Mac, FHA, VA, USDA, or your specific jumbo lender—and every loan needs to fit in their box.

That's it. A box.

Each borrower has to fit into that box using three primary puzzle pieces:

- **Debt-to-Income ratio (DTI)**

- **Loan-to-Value ratio (LTV)**
- **Credit Score**

Overlay those numbers, and you either fit or you don't.

Now, we wish it ended there. But the next level is what we call **overlays**. That's where each individual lender adds their own rules on top of the standard matrix. Why? Because they're managing their own appetite for risk.

We've seen lenders who won't touch a file unless the borrower has a 720+ FICO—even if the program technically allows a 620. Others might require two years of tax returns on a loan where only one year is needed. One lender might allow gift funds from a cousin; another might not.

If you think that's frustrating, imagine being a borrower who submits to one lender, gets denied, and assumes they're not qualified—when really, they just didn't match **that lender's** extra rules.

We've seen it a thousand times. It's not that you're not qualified. It's that your puzzle pieces didn't fit their weird little version of the game.

This is why **working with a good broker** (like us) matters. We don't just shop rates—we shop approval criteria. We know that Lender A might approve your loan with one pay stub, no tax returns, and an appraisal waiver . . . while

Lender B is going to want your entire financial autobiography and a blood sample.

We choose Lender A every time.

Reality Check: Underwriters Are Trained To Assume You're Hiding Something

We love underwriters. They are the backbone of the mortgage industry. But let's be honest—they're trained skeptics.

Their job is to assume you're not telling the full truth.

And unfortunately, they're often right. Mortgage fraud is a real thing. The most common red flag? People lying about **occupancy** to get a lower rate.

It happens constantly. Someone says they're going to live in the home but actually plan to rent it out. That's fraud—and it's one of the biggest things that trips alarms inside underwriting.

Even something as innocent as a married couple buying a house under one spouse's name can raise red flags if their current home isn't being sold.

Why?

Because the algorithm assumes something shady is happening. A divorce. A hidden second home. A clever attempt to avoid a higher rate on an investment property.

If the story doesn't make sense on paper, the underwriter will dig. And dig hard. That's why we say:

"The story must match the math. And the math must match the documents."

If any of those three don't align—boom. Delay. Condition. Denial. Or worse, post-closing audit and repurchase demand.

We've seen it all. Borrowers who thought they were clever. Borrowers who thought their lender wouldn't double-check. Borrowers who assumed "nobody would notice."

Spoiler alert: they noticed.

How We Make Underwriting Easy: Smart Matchmaking

Before we ever run your file through underwriting, we **pre-match you** with the right loan type and lender.

It's matchmaking, really. Your financial DNA has a unique profile—and it needs a lender that says "yes" to people like you.

This is why we don't guess. We run your profile through both **Fannie Mae's DU system** and **Freddie Mac's LP system**. One might approve with fewer documents. One might waive the appraisal. One might like your self-employment history better. We go with that one.

Here's an example:

Same borrower. Same income. Same home.

- Fannie says: 2 years of taxes, full appraisal, full reserves.
- Freddie says: 1 pay stub, no tax returns, appraisal waiver.
  Which one do you want?

Exactly.

Red Flags That Set Off Sirens (And Kill Deals)

Underwriting isn't just paperwork. It's a finely tuned fraud-detection system with a built-in BS meter—and that meter is always running.

We've seen it all.

We've had married couples suddenly qualifying separately . . . while still living together, still sharing bills, still listing each other as emergency contacts. Underwriting doesn't just glance at that and say "weird." It smells smoke and starts looking for fire.

Why? Because we know the play. A couple is splitting up, or one is buying the house solo, in case something goes wrong. But they're not disclosing it. And if there's one thing lenders hate more than fraud, it's **hidden intent**.

It gets worse.

People try to get creative—buying a smaller house while keeping their current one and calling the new one their "primary residence." That's a big one. Maybe your current house is 2,400 square feet, and you're "downsizing" to a 1,200 square foot ranch . . . but you're not selling the old house. Oh, and it's only five miles away. Red flags are screaming.

We're not saying it's impossible. But lenders aren't dumb. Fannie and Freddie know what's up.

They've seen borrowers do this hundreds of times—to skirt the higher rates and down payments that come with second homes or investment properties. It's tempting to just say, "We're moving!" But if that move never happens and they audit the file later . . . your story better hold.

Because here's the truth: **You don't own that rate if you lied to get it.** They can call the loan due.

That's right. If you said you'd occupy the home within 60 days and you didn't, they can force a refinance. Or worse: call the note. That's not a fun letter to get in the mail.

"Your file isn't a story. It's a sworn testimony. And every page better match the truth."

Wild Conditions from the Underwriting Twilight Zone

Let's talk about some of the insane documentation requests we've seen underwriters throw out like confetti at a fraud parade.

We've had an underwriter request **proof of Amazon deliveries** to verify occupancy. Not joking. Amazon Prime became the new electric bill. "Show us you live there" now includes tracking numbers.

How about this: One underwriter wanted a **letter of explanation** for why the borrower's paycheck came in on a Wednesday instead of the typical Friday. True story. Turns out it was a holiday. Still required a letter.

Oh, and our favorite? A borrower once received a condition asking for **the full divorce decree**—not because it was relevant—but because the ex's name showed up in a Venmo transaction on a shared bank statement. That's how deep they go.

It gets crazier when people try to be slick.

We had one borrower—let's call her Sarah—who wanted to buy in Oregon while still owning a place in Virginia. Her plan sounded fine at first: remote work, new partner, fresh start. But when we asked her if she could take occupancy within 60 days, she hesitated.

Red flag.

If that's not your primary residence, then your rate is going to be 1.5–2% higher. And that's fine, as long as you're honest. But if you try to fudge the truth, the whole deal can explode in your face.

And guess what? Fannie Mae doesn't care about your love life. They care about what's on that signed document.

How We Prep Borrowers Like Pros

This is where great loan officers separate themselves from the pack. Anyone can say, "Send me your pay stubs and W-2s." But only pros understand the *why* behind every document.

We don't just ask for paperwork—we build the whole strategy.

Before we ever pull credit, we'll ask the right questions to sniff out potential landmines:

- Are you keeping your current home?
- Are you self-employed or W-2?
- Do you own other properties?
- Do you receive child support or alimony?
- Have you moved jobs in the last 6 months?

These questions aren't just nosy—they're tactical. Because we've seen borrowers spend 60 days on a file that should've been denied on Day 1.

Wanna know the fastest way to derail a deal? **Surprise us.** Don't tell us about your new job that doesn't have a pay history yet. Or the fact that your down payment is coming from grandma's mattress.

We prep borrowers by looking through the lens of every possible underwriter. If your story makes sense and your paperwork backs it up, the file sails through.

If it doesn't?

The loan doesn't close. And we don't get second chances when that happens.

Why "It's Just Paperwork" Is a Lie

We get clients all the time who say, "This should be easy—I make good money, my credit is great."

Fantastic. But that doesn't mean underwriting will be.

Lenders don't care about your intentions. They care about **documentation**. You might be the most financially responsible person in the country, but if your paperwork doesn't match the narrative—we're not getting a green light.

Let's take self-employed borrowers.

We had a borrower last month with a killer business. Money in the bank. Big deposits every month. He figured the loan would be a breeze.

But we pulled tax returns and—surprise—he wrote off everything but oxygen.

On paper, the guy made $12,000 a year. Loan denied.

That's the reality. Income is what's taxed, not what's earned. And lenders use the tax return, not your business checking account.

So what did we do?

We found a solution. We structured the loan based on 12-month bank statements through one of our alternative-doc lenders. We still got him approved—because we knew where to pivot.

And that's what we mean when we say: **Get your paperwork dialed in.**

Red Flags That Make Underwriters Sweat

You know what gets underwriters pacing around the office? Red flags.

Not always fraud. But sometimes? Absolutely fraud.

Let's clear one thing up: Red flags don't automatically kill a deal—but they sure as hell slow it down, raise the blood pressure, and invite a forensic deep dive into your financial soul.

Red Flag #1: The "I Swear It's My Primary" Lie

Here's the scenario: You're buying a second house. Maybe it's smaller, in a different city, and suddenly you're claiming it's your *primary residence*. Meanwhile, you're keeping the 3,000 square foot house with the pool and barbecue grill. Sure. That tracks.

We've seen this move a thousand times. It's the most common occupancy lie in lending—and the most easily caught. Why? Because it's one of the few things lenders keep checking after closing. Not for a week. Not for a month. But for *five years.*

Let that sink in. Fannie and Freddie will audit occupancy for up to **five years** after the loan funds. You said you'd live there? Cool. Prove it—with driver's license, voter registration, utility bills, Amazon shipping address, W-2 update, insurance . . . the whole package.

If you claimed primary and you're not living there, the hammer drops. You'll be forced to refinance at investor rates or—worst-case—they call the loan due in full.

And if it was intentional? That's mortgage fraud. Federal crime. Prosecution-level offense. Just to shave a percent off your rate.

Red Flag #2: "We're Still Married, But . . ."

Here's another one that gets eyebrows raised: a married couple who've always filed jointly, always been on everything together, suddenly separating their financial lives for a new loan.

Only one is applying. They're "still married" but living apart. There's tension in the tax returns. The underwriter's Spidey senses are tingling. Why?

Because this often signals a divorce in motion. Or worse—a fraudulent attempt to qualify separately while hiding liabilities or assets.

Now, sometimes it's legit. We're not saying it isn't. But if you're going solo on the mortgage, be ready to explain it. In writing. With logic. And a paper trail.

Red Flag #3: "I'm Keeping the Big House . . . But Buying a Tiny One"

This one always raises the big red flag: buying a smaller house in worse condition, while "retaining" a nicer home. Then claiming it's your new primary.

That doesn't pass the sniff test.

This is one of the top fraud alerts in the industry—and for good reason. It's almost always someone trying to dodge second-home or investor rate pricing. It's not that the logic is impossible. It's just that it's rarely true.

So the underwriter digs. And if it doesn't make sense? You're either getting a denial or you're signing a statement that makes it crystal clear you understand what you're doing—and what's at stake if you lie.

We've had people walk away when they realize they're being called out. That's a red flag in itself. If you won't explain your plan with clarity and honesty? There's a reason you're looking for a different lender.

The Watch List Is Real

You know what's wild? Brokers across the country all swim in the same pools.

Let's say you come to us, we spot a problem, and we say, "No go. This stinks."

Then you bounce and take your deal to a different broker. Maybe a town over. Maybe the same street.

Guess what? If they also use United Wholesale Mortgage (and 86% of brokers do), your file gets flagged.

We've had clients come crawling back saying, "Did you tell them I was a problem?"

No. We didn't.

But UWM did.

That's how centralized things are. The lender already saw your deal. Already tagged it. Already knows you were trying to game the system.

This isn't paranoia. It's reality.

And if your new lender isn't smart enough to read the signs on your credit report or notice the recent drop-off from another broker, you're dealing with someone who doesn't know what the hell they're doing.

Do yourself a favor: don't try to lie your way to a better loan. It's not worth it. The industry has become too connected, too algorithmically sharp, and too protective of its risk pools to let it slide anymore.

In the end, the paper always tells the truth. And if the story doesn't match the paperwork? You're not getting the keys.

How to Prep for Smooth Approval (aka Kill the Chaos)

Let's shift gears.

You now know the red flags. You know the landmines. So how do you avoid getting flagged in the first place? How do you glide through underwriting like a pro instead of stumbling through it like a rookie?

You prep smarter.

The biggest myth in mortgages? That underwriting is some kind of black magic. It's not. It's math and paper.

More specifically? It's a matrix of loan-to-value, credit score, debt-to-income ratio, and document validation. Plug in the numbers. Submit the proof. That's it.

So here's how we prep our clients so they don't just survive underwriting—they dominate it.

1. Start With the Actual Loan Approval Engine

Before you send over a single tax return, we run your file through Fannie Mae's Desktop Underwriter (DU) and Freddie Mac's Loan Product Advisor (LPA).

Why both?

Because they don't give the same answers. It's like running two apps to compare directions. Sometimes Freddie gives a smoother ride. Sometimes Fannie is stricter. We look for the easier path.

Here's a real example:

- Fannie says: "We want 2 years' tax returns, full appraisal, and 3 months of bank statements."
- Freddie says: "One pay stub, one bank statement, and we'll waive the appraisal."

Same borrower. Same house. Same loan amount. One path is a paper jungle. The other is clean pavement.

Which one do you think we chose?

2. Don't Dump Your Life Story. Wait for the Checklist.

We don't want your entire life in a Dropbox folder before we even know what's needed.

That's not efficient. That's overwhelming.

So here's our system: we get your permission to pull credit; we collect the basics (income, assets, job history); we run the DU/LPA approval; and only then do we send a tailored list of documents you actually need to submit.

It might be 6 documents. It might be 16. But you'll know exactly what's required.

And if something's missing or doesn't look right? We'll ask. But we're not playing guessing games. Everything is intentional.

3. Understand Overlay Land

Many years back, it was a well-known fact in the mortgage industry that Bank of America added overlays—additional guidelines stricter than the base FHA, VA, or conventional rules.

For instance, they required a **720 credit score minimum** for *any* loan.

Even FHA. Even VA. Even if the base guidelines allowed for lower.

Why? Because that was their internal risk tolerance.

As brokers, we don't play that game.

We go where the client's profile fits best. One lender may allow 620 on FHA with 50% DTI. Another won't. One lender may want two years' tax returns for self-employed borrowers. Another will take one year.

You don't need to fight the system. You just need to know which system to choose.

We navigate that for you.

4. Prepare for the Weird Requests (They're Coming)

Even the cleanest files can attract some bizarre conditions. Lenders are infamous for asking for things that sound ridiculous. But we don't complain—we anticipate.

Here are real requests we've seen:

- A letter explaining why a client's mother lives with them.
- A signed statement promising not to buy another property in the next 6 months.
- Proof that a 20-year-old credit card was not opened fraudulently.

Wild? Yes. But if you're ready for it, you just knock it out and move on.

The difference between a delayed closing and an on-time one is how fast you respond to these curveballs.

5. The 90% Rule

Here's a rule of thumb we live by:

90% of underwriting delays happen because the borrower wasn't properly prepped.

Let that sink in.

It's not the underwriter's fault. It's not the lender's. It's that the original loan officer didn't dig deep enough or anticipate what would be needed.

We're not those loan officers.

We operate under the "no surprises" rule. We'd rather ask for one extra document upfront than stall a closing because someone "forgot" a bank statement.

Lesson from the Trenches: Underwriting Isn't the End. It's the Start.

Even if your loan gets cleared to close, you are still **accountable**.

Fannie and Freddie have **up to five years** to perform an audit. If you've misrepresented anything—especially occupancy—they can:

- Demand immediate refinance

- Hit you with penalties
- Flag your name in the system
- Refer the case for mortgage fraud prosecution

And yes—**occupancy fraud is a federal crime**.

Let that sit with you.

You think lenders don't follow up? They do. Quietly. After you've relaxed. That's when they come knocking.

The No-Surprise Playbook

By now, you get it: surprises kill deals. Especially in underwriting.

But here's the good news: almost every surprise can be neutralized **before** it ever becomes a problem.

We call it the No-*Surprise Playbook*. And if you're working with a pro, it should already be part of the game plan.

Your Pre-Approval Isn't a Golden Ticket

Let's be real for a second.

Pre-approvals are often handed out like Costco samples—easy to get, and usually not the full meal. If your lender didn't verify income, assets, and credit with hard data, you're not really approved.

You're just *pre-dreaming.*

Too many buyers fall into the trap of "my lender said I'm good." Then they find a home, go under contract, and suddenly, underwriting throws a wrench in the machine.

Why?

Because no one opened the hood.

The Ultimate Document Checklist (Tailored to You)

Forget the 20-item generic lists floating around online. The right checklist is customized to your loan type, job type, and credit profile.

That said, here's a solid starting point for most borrowers:

Standard Employment

- 2 most recent pay stubs
- Most recent 2 years W-2s
- Most recent 1–2 bank statements (all pages, even blank ones)
- Government-issued ID

Self-Employed or 1099

- 2 most recent years of personal and business tax returns (all schedules)
- Year-to-date profit & loss statement
- 2 months of the most recent business bank statements
- Business license or CPA letter

Rental Property Owners

- Lease agreements
- Mortgage statements for all properties
- Insurance declarations
- HOA statements, if applicable

Additional Items Based on Scenario

- Divorce decree (if applicable)
- Child support/alimony documentation
- Gift letter (if funds are gifted)
- Letter of explanation for credit inquiries or job gaps
- Work-from-home documentation (for remote buyers)
- Relocation letters (if changing states)

And again—this isn't guesswork.

Once we run your scenario through Fannie Mae or Freddie Mac's AUS (Automated Underwriting System), it literally tells us **exactly** what will be required for final approval.

We follow the machine, not a hunch.

Why We Don't Ask for More Than We Need

Here's where we do things differently.

We've worked in the retail world, where banks ask for **everything** up front. Not because they need it—but because they want a fully stacked file *just in case.*

But that's lazy lending. And it's exhausting for you.

In the wholesale broker world, we pull exactly what your approval requires—nothing more, nothing less. That means:

- You submit fewer documents
- You close faster
- You avoid overexposing your file to unnecessary scrutiny

This precision comes from experience and knowing how to interpret the results of your AUS findings.

It's also why we often run your file through **both** Fannie and Freddie's systems. Sometimes one requires less documentation or offers better pricing. Sometimes one waives the appraisal and the other doesn't.

We don't guess.

We run both and pick the smarter path.

Letters of Explanation: Your Silent Killer or Secret Weapon

One letter—just one—can make or break a deal.

We've seen borrowers write rambling, defensive essays explaining job gaps or late payments that ended up triggering more questions than they answered.

Don't do that.

Every Letter of Explanation should be:

- **Short:** One paragraph, two at most.
- **Factual:** No drama. No excuses.
- **Clear:** Address the issue directly, then move on.

Bad:
"I was going through a lot in my personal life and didn't know what to do, so I just ignored the calls and fell behind. It was a really rough time, and I hope you understand."

Better:
"In July 2023, I was unemployed for 30 days due to company downsizing. I've since secured stable full-time employment and maintained all accounts in good standing."

Underwriters are trained to spot red flags in *tone*, not just content. Keep it clean, tight, and factual. We help our clients write these every day. It matters more than you think.

The Final Truth: Underwriting Is Not the Enemy

It's easy to hate underwriting.

They ask weird questions. They request documents you already sent. They don't care that your cousin's dog's surgery cost $2,000.

But they're not the enemy.

They're the bouncer at the door of the financial club. Their job is to keep the system from collapsing under fraud, misrepresentation, or sloppy documentation.

If you're working with someone who understands the system—and prepares you accordingly—underwriting becomes a handshake, not a battle.

We've closed thousands of loans, and we can tell you: **the smoothest files win.**

Finish Like a Pro (Or Watch the Clock Explode)

Let's talk about closing day.

You've done the work. You picked the home. Negotiated the price. Found the lender. Got the rate. Your approval is in, and the finish line is in sight.

But then—BOOM. Something stupid derails the whole thing.

We've seen loans delayed for **seven days** because a borrower forgot to include *page* 6 of their bank statement. That page was blank. Nothing on it. But the underwriter flagged the missing page, the processor emailed, and by the time the borrower responded (from their weekend in Mexico), the closing had to be rescheduled.

That's real.

And that's why we don't celebrate early.

Until the ink is dry, *everything counts.*

The Most Common Paperwork Mistakes That Blow Up Closings

Let's call these what they are: preventable landmines.

1. **Missing Pages on Statements**
   Yes, even blank ones. If the PDF says "Page 1 of 6," we need all 6. Underwriters aren't playing games.

2. **Unreadable Documents**
   Photos of screens, folded pay stubs, screenshots with missing totals—they all slow the train.
3. **Changed Job or Income Mid-Process**
   You got a new job offer? Cool. Tell us **first.** Don't assume. It might require re-approval.
4. **Deposits Not Documented**
   Zelle from Grandma? Venmo from a buddy? Any large deposit over standard income needs a paper trail.
5. **Late Disclosures**
   If you delay signing disclosures or initial documents, you start a domino effect on the timeline.
6. **"Surprise" Credit Activity**
   You bought furniture on credit during escrow? That innocent $4,000 card swipe just killed your DTI. Game over.

The 72-Hour Rule

Want to close smoothly?

Nothing should change in the 72 hours before closing.

No job changes.
No new credit pulls.
No balance transfers.
No major bank movements.
No calls to your cousin Larry asking for last-minute cash.

Lock it in. Coast. Let the process finish clean.

This Is Not Paranoia. It's Math.

Mortgage underwriting is algorithmic. It's black-and-white. If your income, credit, or assets change even slightly, your automated approval might disappear—and you don't get to argue with a software engine.

Once that happens? It's a full re-run of your file. New disclosures. New lock. New rate. New problems.

We've seen buyers lose their dream home over a $300 Target credit card they opened to get 5% off a vacuum.

Don't be that person.

Mindset of a Mortgage Ninja

By Rule 8, you're no longer just a buyer. You're a strategic operator on a financial mission.

Think like a ninja:

- Light on your feet
- Silent with your moves
- Precise with your strikes

Every document you submit is a weapon. Every day you respond quickly is a win. Every unknown you neutralize early is a step closer to victory.

You are not hoping for approval.
You are engineering it.

We Run Our Files Like We're Betting Our Own Homes

Here's our promise: when we prep your file, we treat it like our own. We don't guess. We don't push fluff. We don't just "see what happens."

We dig deep, surface the flags, and build your file to *pass audit standards before we ever submit.*

Because if your file gets audited three years from now—and yes, it happens—we want you to be bulletproof.

Mortgage Club Confession (Extended Truth)

We once had a borrower who swore up and down that their new purchase would be their primary home. They kept their old home. Said they were going to rent it. But we knew the numbers didn't make sense.

Still, they insisted. Wrote a letter. Said all the right things.

Three months later, we got a call from the lender:

The borrower had never moved.

Amazon deliveries, utilities, insurance—all still tied to the old house.
Audit triggered. Fraud suspected. The borrower was forced to refinance—and paid $9,200 in fees and penalties.

The original loan had a 5.875% rate.
The new loan came in at 7.25%.
All because they "forgot to move in."

That wasn't just expensive. That was federal.

Your Final Checklist: Rule 8 Recap

Here's how to crush your paperwork and prevent surprises:

- Get a **custom checklist** based on your actual AUS results.
- Send **all pages** of every doc—no screenshots.
- Don't change **anything** mid-loan without talking to us first.
- Ask us to **run both Fannie and Freddie** for the best pricing and fewer conditions.
- Write tight, factual **letters of explanation.**
- Avoid **red flags** like second home fraud or sketchy occupancy claims.

- Assume your loan **will be audited** in the next five years.
- Don't take shortcuts. They're expensive in the long run.

That's Rule 8.

Get your paperwork dialed in, so there are no surprises. Because in this game, precision isn't extra. It's everything. Welcome to Mortgage Club.

RULE #9:

Underwriting is War. Keep Your Cool.

Mortgage Club Confession:
The Doobie-Elephant File

-By Tim Rhey

You think you're ready.

You sent the paperwork, got pre-approved, found the house, signed the contract, and popped the champagne.

Then, suddenly—bam—your loan file gets flagged.

The underwriter just issued 17 conditions. You're confused. Your realtor's panicking. And someone somewhere just uttered the word "denied."

Welcome to underwriting.

We once had a borrower—we'll call him Chad—who ran a completely legal cannabis dispensary in Colorado. Profitable, tax-paying, squeaky-clean books. But because of the federal gray area, one underwriter kicked the file back with the comment: "Concerned about industry."

To make it worse, Chad's business partner—an artist—had deposited a $4,000 sculpture commission into their joint account two weeks prior. The note on the check?

"Doobie Elephant."

I wish I were kidding.

The underwriter flagged it. Demanded an explanation.

So we drafted what might be the greatest Letter of Explanation in mortgage history, titled:

"Regarding the Doobie-Elephant Deposit."

It passed. Chad got the loan.

The moral? Underwriting isn't just black and white. It's a wild, bureaucratic jungle—and your guide better have a map.

• • • • • • • • • • • • • • •

What Underwriters Are Really Looking For

Let's break the mystery.

Underwriters are not monsters. They're compliance experts hired to protect the lender. Their job is to confirm—without a shadow of a doubt—that:

1. You are who you say you are.
2. You can afford the loan.
3. You're not laundering drug money.
4. Your documents match the loan program guidelines.
5. The property is suitable collateral.

They're checking every corner of your file to make sure the loan can be sold or insured because behind every mortgage is either Fannie Mae, Freddie Mac, FHA, VA, or a private investor. If that investor finds one crack in the foundation, they can refuse to buy it—leaving the lender stuck.

So the underwriter's mindset isn't "Let's approve this buyer."

It's: **"Can I defend this file in an audit 3 years from now?"**

When you understand that, the weird questions make more sense.

The Emotional Roller Coaster of Conditions

There are three types of underwriting conditions:

1. **Prior-to-Doc Conditions (PTDs)** - Must be cleared before loan documents are sent.
2. **Prior-to-Funding Conditions (PTFs)** - Cleared just before closing and funding.
3. **Post-Close Conditions** - Cleared by the lender after you've closed.

PTDs are the most intense.

They may ask for letters of explanation, updated pay stubs, large deposit sourcing, gift letters, divorce decrees, or clarification on your 401(k) loan. Some of it will seem totally irrelevant.

It isn't.

It's the underwriter's job to leave no gaps.

But here's where it gets hard for buyers:

It feels personal.

You've sent your life story. You've been vulnerable. And now someone you've never met is questioning it all.

That's where panic sets in.

> *"Underwriting doesn't test your finances. It tests your patience."*

Letters of Explanation (LOX): The Secret Weapon

Ah yes—the infamous **LOX**. (No, not the salmon kind.)

A Letter of Explanation is exactly what it sounds like: a short, factual note that clarifies something in your file.

The key to writing one?

Don't overshare. Don't get emotional. Don't try to justify. Just explain.

Bad LOX:

"I was late on my credit card because my ex stole money, my car broke down, and then my boss fired me, and I had a meltdown."

Good LOX:

"The payment due 3/2/23 was made late due to an unexpected car repair. The account has remained current since."

See the difference?

We've written hundreds of LOXs. Some are two lines long. Others are full-page statements with supporting documents. The goal is simple:

Give the underwriter enough clarity to check the box and move on.

How to Not Freak Out

Let's be clear:

Almost every loan gets conditions.

Even perfect borrowers get flagged. It's part of the process.

The worst thing you can do is:

- Stop responding.
- Argue with your lender.
- Complain to your realtor.
- Spiral emotionally.

Instead:

- Respond quickly.
- Stay factual.
- Ask questions if confused.
- Let your loan officer quarterback the response.

Most underwriting "emergencies" aren't emergencies at all. They're fixable—if you keep calm and communicate.

Real Stories of Last-Minute Saves

We had a borrower—first-time buyer, great job, W-2 income—whose dad gifted him $40K for the down payment.

He sent the gift letter. Check.

Sent the dad's bank statement. Check.

But the underwriter flagged one weird line: a $12K wire into Dad's account two weeks prior.

"Source this deposit," they said.

Turns out it was an inheritance from an uncle in Canada. So now we had to:

- Get documentation from Canada
- Translate the will due to being written in French
- Prove the transfer into the dad's account was legitimate
- Prove the gift from dad to son was clean

Four layers deep—just to clear a gift.

It took 48 hours and about a dozen emails. But we got it done.

The loan closed on time.

And the buyer never knew how close it came to derailing.

That's what we do.

The Underwriting Survival Plan

Here's your roadmap:

1. Expect Conditions

Don't be surprised when they ask for more stuff. They always do.

2. Document Everything

Keep a paper trail—especially for large deposits, gifts, or job changes.

3. Don't Change Anything Mid-Process

No new cars. No job switches. No surprise cash deposits.

4. Answer Every Request Clearly

Short, factual, and with supporting docs.

5. Let Your Lender Fight For You

Some conditions are unreasonable. We'll push back if needed.

6. Stay Emotionally Detached

This is business. Don't take it personally.

Mortgage Club Action Takeaways: Rule 9

1. **Know the Underwriting Mindset**
   It's about defensibility, not fairness.
2. **Master the LOX**
   Short. Clear. Factual. No drama.
3. **Expect Conditions**
   They're normal, not a red flag.
4. **Trust Your Loan Team**
   We've danced this dance before.

5. **Don't Panic**
   Emotions cloud judgment. Stay the course.

Final Word

Underwriting is where weak loans die . . . and strong files get sharpened.

It's uncomfortable. It's frustrating. It tests your patience and your ability to stay calm under pressure.

But here's the truth:

If your loan team knows what they're doing—and you stay engaged—there is almost nothing underwriting can throw at you that we can't navigate.

So breathe.

Respond.

And let us handle the rest.

Because at Mortgage Club, we don't fold under pressure.

We clear to close.

RULE #10:

Closing Day: Smile, Sign, Survive.

Mortgage Club Confession
"Deadbeat Dad and the $125K Surprise"
– Rich Hanlin

The closing table should be the victory lap. But for one borrower I'll never forget, it became a full-blown crash and burn.

This was after the housing collapse, sometime around 2012. The rules were changing, and new protections were being added to prevent last-minute disasters. Unfortunately, the past still had a few punches to throw.

The borrower was doing a cash-out refinance. He had gone through the entire process—credit, appraisal, underwriting—all the way to closing day. His goal was to pull out $100,000 in equity. No issues . . . or so we thought.

In California, we do a final title "date-down" check before closing—essentially reviewing the public records from the last recorded title activity up to the current date.

This is the moment where things can still go sideways.

And they did.

This borrower had told us—sworn to us—he had no child support or alimony obligations. But that final title search pulled up multiple active liens. Not just one or two. Several. From different counties.

See, he misunderstood the question. When we asked if he owed child support or alimony, he thought we were asking only about his current county.

He failed to mention the three other counties that had slapped him with legal judgments totaling $125,000.

That's right. Deadbeat dad status. Unpaid. Undisclosed. And now, unavoidable.

We couldn't fund the loan. The equity was gone. The borrower was out. Everyone involved—loan officer, processor, title agent—had their time wasted, all because he hadn't been honest, or worse, didn't understand the stakes.

• • • • • • • • • • • • • • •

That's why Rule 10 matters. Mastering the closing table isn't just about knowing where to sign—it's about understanding that *nothing* should be a surprise.

Since 2012, the federal regulations have required a loan estimate up front and a closing disclosure at the end. What you see is what you get—unless *you* change something.

If something does change in your file and it impacts your numbers? You're getting a new disclosure and a new 3-day waiting period.

No more last-minute bait-and-switch. No more "I didn't know." The system was built to protect you—if you're honest, prepared, and working with someone who knows how to guide you through it.

Lesson: There are no secrets at the closing table. Just facts. And consequences.

The Closing Table Isn't the End—It's the Boss Battle

You made it.

After weeks of uploading documents, choosing loan terms, battling appraisal nerves, and calculating every penny . . . you've reached the final boss: the closing table.

But here's the thing—closing is not just signing papers and grabbing keys.

It's a minefield.

And if you don't walk into that room prepared—with eyes wide open—you can get hit with:

- Wire fraud that drains your bank account
- Surprise fees that suddenly appear from the shadows
- Confusing title documents you didn't know you agreed to
- Delays because someone forgot a signature or ID

- Insurance mistakes that sabotage your monthly payment

This chapter is your armor.

We're going to teach you exactly what happens at closing, what to read, what to ignore, how to protect your money, and how to walk out as a homeowner with zero regrets.

We'll break down the chaos we've seen—and how we saved the day.

And we'll wrap it all up with a **Closing Day Checklist** that will make you a black belt in closing room jiu-jitsu.

Let's go.

Topic 1: What Actually Happens at Closing?

First, let's clarify the lingo.

Some people call it the "signing." Others say "closing." In most cases, both are accurate—but what it means can depend on your state.

Here's what closing typically looks like:

You show up at an escrow office, a title company, or a real estate attorney's office. You bring your photo ID. You sit down with a notary. And in front of you is a stack of loan documents as thick as a phone book.

The notary will verify your identity, explain what you're signing (in general terms), and walk you through the paperwork.

This is where you *officially* agree to the loan terms and ownership transfer.

Depending on whether you're in a **wet** or **dry** funding state, the timing of money movement and recording varies:

- **Dry Funding States** (e.g., California): You sign the documents, and then the lender funds the loan after reviewing them. This can take 1–2 days.
- **Wet Funding States** (e.g., Colorado, Texas, Georgia): The money is already at the title company. You sign, they record the documents, and boom—you're officially closed, often same-day.

Now here's the twist most people don't realize:

If you're doing a refinance on your *primary residence*, federal law requires a **three-day waiting period** even after signing. That means you don't "close" until that rescission period expires.

If it's a purchase or an investment property? No waiting. You're done the moment funding hits and title records the deal.

Wire Fraud, Last-Minute Costs, and Dodging Landmines

Fraud isn't a maybe—it's a certainty if you're not careful. And it's worse than ever.

In the mortgage world, cybercriminals don't need to hack systems. They just need to trick *you*.

They use a tactic called **phishing**—spelled with a "ph"—which means sending fake emails that look legit but are designed to intercept your information.

One of the most dangerous targets? Your wire instructions.

They'll pose as your escrow agent, lender, or even your real estate agent. You get a friendly email saying: "Please wire your closing funds to this account."

Except it's not the right account. It's a criminal's. And once you send it? That money is gone.

Forever.

That's why every reputable title company will now *require* a verbal call to confirm wire instructions. If you don't get that call, initiate it yourself.

Always call the number you received directly from your escrow officer early in the process—*not* the one from a last-minute email.

And never wire funds without confirming by voice.

Next Up: Last-Minute Costs.

This is where people get blindsided.

- Suddenly, your homeowner's insurance quote is off by $800.
- The title company discovers you need flood insurance—yesterday.
- There's a $300 document recording fee you didn't plan for.

We've seen all of these happen.

Here's how we fix it:

1. **Insurance Deductibles:** Many people default to low deductibles ($250–$500), which raises premiums. If you increase your deductible to $2,500, your insurance premium can drop dramatically—sometimes by 50% or more.
2. **Recast Payment Strategy:** If you're short on funds at closing, we can sometimes restructure the loan or shift funds within allowable tolerances.
3. **Verify Title Fees Early:** We do a pre-closing fee audit with every client. Most lenders don't.

Our goal? **No surprises at the table.**

Title, Escrow, and the Secrets Buried in the Paperwork

Let's shine a light on the most misunderstood players in the homebuying game: **title and escrow**.

Most borrowers glaze over when they hear those words. But if you want to win at the mortgage table—and avoid losing thousands—you need to understand what title and escrow actually do.

Escrow is the neutral middleman. They hold the money. They collect your loan documents. They follow the instructions from all sides—buyer, seller, lender—and ensure the deal happens by the book.

Title is the detective. Their job is to make sure no one else can claim ownership of your home.

They dig deep:

- Are there unpaid liens?
- Does a contractor from 2018 still have a bill on file?
- Is there an old ex on title that no one told you about?
- Is the seller even *legally* allowed to sell this house?

Once title verifies the property is clean, they issue a **title insurance policy**—a guarantee that you now own the home, free and clear.

You'll pay for this title insurance at closing. It's not optional. But it's vital.

Here's the catch: Some shady title companies sneak in padded fees. Courier fees. Email fees. "File storage" fees. Nonsense.

We've seen title companies charge $800 for a mobile notary that costs $125.

That's why you must **read your closing disclosure.**

Compare it to your loan estimate. Ask your loan officer, "Why did this title fee change?"

If they don't know—or they tell you to "just sign it"—you've got a problem.

In the next part, we'll break down closing day chaos . . . and how we fix it like pros.

Closing Day Chaos: Real Stories, Real Fixes

Let's be real.

As much as we prep, organize, and color-code the entire transaction, **something always goes sideways on closing day.**

Not every time. But enough to keep us humble.

Let's talk about the chaos. And more importantly—how we fix it.

STORY #1: The Insurance Bombshell

We had a buyer in Florida. New construction. Gorgeous property. Everything was rolling smoothly.

Then, closing day hits—and the insurance quote comes in **$9,400 higher** than expected.

Why? The agent forgot to factor in wind mitigation and hurricane protection. That oversight blew up the escrow amount and the monthly payment.

The borrower panicked. She was ready to walk.

How we fixed it:

We jumped on a call with the insurance provider, re-ran quotes using higher deductibles and accurate protection credits, and dropped the premium by over $6,000.

But here's the real kicker: she had another quote in her inbox the entire time from 3 weeks prior—**$5,200 cheaper**—and forgot about it.

Moral: Don't just trust one quote. Ask your lender to help vet them *before* closing day.

STORY #2: Missing Funds, Missing Mind

Another time, a young couple went to closing . . . and realized they hadn't wired the rest of their down payment.

They swore they had. But nope. Their bank put a hold on the wire due to daily limits. The funds would arrive the following Monday.

It was Friday.

Cue the cold sweats.

The seller was already packed. The moving truck was in the driveway. The listing agent was panicking.

How we fixed it:

Because we had a relationship with the title company and knew the lender was flexible, we negotiated a "partial funding hold." They signed as scheduled, and we instructed the title office to hold the file until funds arrived on Monday.

They got the keys by Tuesday. And their marriage survived.

STORY #3: The Power of Reading Your Documents

This one's simple but shocking.

A client in Texas was reviewing her closing docs and noticed that the deed of trust listed an HOA she had *never* agreed to.

Turns out, the seller had added a new community enhancement fee to the subdivision. And nobody flagged it.

It would've added **$117 a month** forever.

She stopped signing.

How we fixed it:

We froze the closing, had title re-run the CC&Rs (community rules), and negotiated with the HOA to waive the startup fee and adjust the monthly amount based on her property's square footage.

It delayed closing by one day—but saved her over $12,000 long-term.

"Closing day doesn't care how smooth your deal was—if you're not paying attention at the end, it can all unravel in 10 minutes."

The 7 Documents That Actually Matter (Read These—Not All 187 Pages of the Loan Docs)

Let's be honest.

Nobody reads the entire loan package at closing. Not even attorneys. If someone tells you they read every page, they either have no kids or no idea what they're reading.

But here's what you *should* read. These 7 documents hold the power. They're the heartbeat of your loan. And they'll reveal—very quickly—if something is wrong.

1. **The Closing Disclosure (CD)**
   This is your final receipt. The real deal.

It outlines:

- Your final loan amount
- Interest rate
- Monthly payment (including taxes, insurance, HOA)
- All fees (lender, title, escrow, third-party)
- Amount due at closing

What to look for:

- Did your rate change?
- Are fees higher than what was on your Loan Estimate?

- Does your cash to close match what your lender told you?

Red flag: If you see fees that weren't disclosed before, **pause**. You have the right to question—and even delay—if something feels off.

2. **The Note**
   This is your promise to pay. It's the "IOU" for your mortgage.

What to check:

- Interest rate
- Loan term (30 years? 15 years?)
- Prepayment penalties (there shouldn't be any)

Look for the words "Fixed Rate Note" at the top. If it says "Adjustable Rate Note," and that's not what you agreed to—*do not sign.*

3. **The Deed of Trust (or Mortgage)**
   This secures the loan to the property. It's recorded with your county.

Key things to spot:

- Your name and property address are correct
- It lists the correct lender

- Look for "Planned Unit Development" box—this is where HOA obligations hide

4. **First Payment Letter**
   This tells you when and where to make your first payment.

Check:

- Due date
- Amount
- Payment address or online portal instructions

Pro tip: Set up autopay immediately after this. One missed payment—even by accident—can crush your credit.

5. **Escrow Account Disclosure**
   This breaks down how your lender will handle taxes and insurance moving forward.

Watch for:

- Monthly escrow amount
- Cushion amount (they're allowed to collect a 2-month buffer)
- Annual analysis assumptions

If your taxes or insurance were under-quoted, your escrow account will go negative next year—and your payment will jump. Ask questions now.

6. **Title Insurance Policy**
   This confirms your ownership—and protects you against past ownership issues.

Important: Make sure **your name is spelled correctly.** You'd be shocked at how many policies have the wrong buyer name or a missing middle initial, which causes issues later when you sell.

7. **Signature/ID Affidavit**
   This one confirms who you are and that you go by the names listed.

If you see a name you don't recognize—say something. Mistakes happen during data entry. You don't want someone else's alias tied to your mortgage.

Hot Take:
The rest of the documents? Legal fluff. Necessary for compliance, but rarely worth more than a skim.

Our advice: Ask your loan officer to highlight these 7 documents at signing. You'll look like a pro, avoid mistakes, and save your sanity.

The Ultimate Closing Day Checklist (So You Don't Blow It in the Final Hour)

You're almost there.

But before you grab the keys and pop the bubbly, let's make sure you're walking into the closing table like a total boss—not a confused first-timer with clammy hands and zero questions.

Here's the definitive Closing Day Checklist.

1. ID, Baby. Don't Forget It.

Bring **two** forms of valid identification.
At minimum:

- A government-issued photo ID (driver's license, passport, or military ID)
- A second form (Social Security card, credit card with name, utility bill, etc.)

Why two?
Because if your name has changed or doesn't match exactly, they may require a second proof. And no, your Costco card doesn't count.

**2. Confirm the Wire Instructions—With Your Voice

Like we covered earlier, do **not** trust email for wiring money. Call the escrow or title company *at their verified number* and ask:

"Can you confirm the wire instructions before I send funds?"

If they don't recognize the wiring info you were given, you just avoided a nightmare.

3. Triple Check the Cash-to-Close Number

Your lender should've given you the exact amount you need to bring to closing—either to wire beforehand or bring via cashier's check (depending on the title company's rules).

Tip:
Always round up slightly in your wire. Overpayments can be refunded, but underpayments delay closings.

4. Block Off Enough Time

Closings usually take **45 to 60 minutes**, but we've seen some stretch to two hours, especially when:

- The notary is chatty
- There are errors that need fixing
- You ask lots of (good) questions

Pro Tip:

Avoid scheduling closing back-to-back with something else. You want time to breathe and focus.

5. Know the 7 Docs That Matter

(From Part 5—go back and review if needed.)
These are the only documents you need to truly **read**:

1. Closing Disclosure
2. Note
3. Deed of Trust
4. First Payment Letter
5. Escrow Disclosure
6. Title Insurance Policy
7. Signature/ID Affidavit

Everything else? Glance and sign—unless something seems wildly off.

6. Ask These Questions at the Table

Even if you feel confident, ask your escrow officer or notary:

- "Are there any last-minute changes I should know about?"
- "Is my first payment date still correct?"
- "Can I get a digital copy of everything today?"
- "Is there anything that looks different from the CD?"

You'll come across as smart and aware. And if there's a hidden mistake? You just gave yourself a lifeline.

7. Read the HOA Box

In the deed of trust, there's a small section that confirms whether the home is in a **Planned Unit Development** (PUD).

Translation?
That means an HOA is involved—and there are rules, fees, and sometimes surprise assessments.

Don't skip this.
We've seen borrowers discover $300 monthly HOA fees *at closing.*

8. Don't Celebrate Until the Deal Records

Just because you've signed doesn't mean you're done.

Especially in dry funding states (like California), recording happens **after** closing, usually the next day.

So don't schedule movers, painters, or contractors for right after signing unless you have confirmation that **funding has occurred and the deed has recorded.**

Mini Case Study:
A client once scheduled her movers, dog groomer, pool guy, and furniture delivery **on closing day.**

Funding got delayed due to a missed signature.

The dog got shampooed.
The movers got paid to wait.
The client got a stress ulcer.

Lesson: Chill until it's 100% official.

Closing Chaos, Real Stories, and Your Final Mortgage Club Orders

Closing day chaos isn't rare. It's common.
Here's what it actually looks like when things go sideways—and how we've pulled borrowers out of the fire.

Case #1: The Wire Fraud That Almost Was

A buyer in California got a legitimate-looking email from "titlecompanysecure@gmail.com."

Looked normal. Sounded polite.
Had their name, address, loan amount—everything.

The email asked for a wire of $86,000.

They almost did it.

At the last second, they remembered our warning and called us.

That email was fake.

And they were 30 seconds away from losing everything.

We sent the correct wire instructions. They closed safely the next day.

Lesson: Trust your gut. Confirm everything with a voice call. If something feels off, stop and ask.

Case #2: The Ghost HOA

Client gets to closing and sees a random $158/month HOA fee on the CD.

They had no idea. Agent never mentioned it. We hadn't seen it either.

Turns out the seller's agent didn't disclose the full HOA details. Title missed it until the end.

What did we do?

We paused closing. Got the full HOA docs. Reviewed them with the buyer. Then, negotiated a **$3,000 seller credit** for the oversight.

Lesson: Read the deed. Look for HOA or PUD boxes. Ask early. Don't assume anything.

Case #3: The Missing Spouse

Sounds like a Netflix thriller, right?

In this case, the borrower was separated, but still legally married. The spouse wasn't on the loan or contract.

But in their state? **Both names had to be on title** unless there was a signed legal waiver.

Nobody caught it.

At closing, the title rep paused everything. "Where's your spouse?"

We had to find the spouse. Fast.
They agreed to sign. But it delayed funding by three days.

Lesson: If you're married—even if separated—tell your lender. Rules vary by state. Don't let emotions derail your deal.

Case #4: The Underwire Close

This one's personal.

A borrower wore the wrong bra to closing. Not a joke.

Her ID was flagged because the airport-style notary scanner picked up wiring in her undergarments and thought it was an identity mismatch.

She had to go home, change clothes, and return.

We now add: **"Wear simple clothes with no metal for notary."**

Ridiculous? Yes.
But it happened.

Final Orders: Your Mortgage Club Commandments for Closing

Let's burn these into your brain.

1. **Never wire money from an email.**
   Voice-confirm with escrow—every time.
2. **Read your closing disclosure like your life depends on it.**
   Because financially, it kinda does.
3. **Don't bring surprises to closing.**
   Cash-to-close? Insurance? Spouse info? All needs to be buttoned up beforehand.
4. **You don't have to read all 120 pages.**
   Just know which 7 documents matter.
5. **Schedule closing early in the day.**
   If anything goes wrong, you'll have time to fix it before recording deadlines.
6. **Ask questions—even if you feel dumb.**
   We'd rather you feel silly now than regretful later.

7. **Don't schedule movers until you get confirmation that recording happened.**
   Yes, even if your agent says, "You're good."

"Closing day is where amateurs get burned and pros get paid. Know the game. Read the room. Trust no email." —Mortgage Club Manual, Section X

RECAP: Rule 10 – Master the Closing Table

You made it to the finish line. But here's the truth:

The closing table isn't the end. It's the final exam. And just like any final, you either pass with clarity and calm—or you panic and pay for it later.

Here's what we covered in this no-fluff, no-nonsense chapter:

What Actually Happens at Closing

- **Wet states** fund same-day.
- **Dry states** wait for funding after document review.
- **Refinances on primary homes** require a 3-day waiting period.
- You'll meet with a notary, show your ID, and sign 100+ pages. (Only 5 really matter—more on that below.)

Wire Fraud is Real. Don't Be a Headline.

- Criminals are *phishing* your email.
- They spoof escrow or lender emails with fake wire instructions.
- One click and $80,000 vanishes. Forever.
- **ALWAYS voice-confirm wire instructions. No exceptions.**

Last-Minute Costs Will Sneak Up If You Let Them

- Surprise HOA dues.
- Escrow "storage" fees.
- Insurance premiums that just doubled. We've seen it all. And we've fixed it all. You must read the **final closing disclosure**. Know what changed. Ask why.

Title and Escrow Are Quiet Power Players

- Title makes sure you *actually own* the house.
- Escrow keeps all parties honest.
- But both can pad fees if you're not watching. Compare final title fees to your loan estimate. Push back if something smells fishy.

Chaos Happens. Be Ready.

We've dealt with:

- Forgotten spouses
- Mystery HOAs
- Signings ruined by metal underwire bras (yep, really)
- Last-minute flood insurance
- Missing documents
- International closings with 4-hour time zone delays

Pro tip: Leave time. Stay calm. Bring your ID. Don't assume. Ask.

Your Closing Day Checklist

1. Photo ID
2. Confirm wire instructions *by voice*
3. Review your final CD line-by-line
4. Double-check your insurance premium and deductible
5. Ask if HOA or flood insurance applies
6. Know the five key docs: Note, Deed, CD, First Payment Notice, Escrow
7. Leave at least an hour to sign
8. Don't bring kids, dogs, or distractions
9. Don't schedule movers until recording is confirmed
10. Ask for help—one question can save you $5,000

Remember:

"The closing table is the last place to zone out. You've come this far—read everything, trust no email, and leave with keys *and* confidence."

RULE #11:

Don't Feed the Interest Monster — Refi & Payoff Strategies That Work

Mortgage Club Confession: "Do you really need 30 credit cards?"

-By Tim Rhey

Let me tell you about a client I'll call Steve.

Steve was in his early 40s, had a decent job, smart guy—but like a lot of Americans, he was in survival mode.

He was selling his home and buying a new one, planning to use the $100,000 he'd net from the sale as the full down payment on his next place.

It all seemed pretty straightforward . . . until we looked under the hood.

Because hidden behind the nice W-2s and the fresh home listing was something much heavier:

Steve had over 30 credit cards.

Most maxed out.
All bleeding him dry.

"I'm just making minimums until I can get this new mortgage done," he said.

Which, to translate, means:
"I'm losing sleep and slowly dying inside."

His minimum payments alone were eating up over $2,000 a month. That's just to stay afloat. No momentum. No progress. Just . . . treading water.

And that's when we paused the whole deal.

Not to stop it—but to flip it.

Instead of applying the full $100K toward the down payment, we restructured the game plan:

- $80K toward the down payment
- $20K toward paying off all the high-interest credit cards

Yes, it meant his new mortgage was $20K higher, and yes, that raised his mortgage payment by about $450/month.

But...

He eliminated $2,000/month in credit card payments.

Let's do the math together:

- $450 mortgage
  – $2,000 credit card payments
  = Net monthly savings: $1,550

That's not just a win—that's a massive financial U-turn.

• • • • • • • • • • • • • • •

Mortgage Club Confession:
Paying down high-interest debt with low-interest mortgage money is not selling out—it's buying freedom.

Don't give all your cash to your house while Visa and Mastercard own your paycheck.

Smart payoff strategies will beat pride—and interest—every time.

Steve called me a few months later.

"I actually feel like I can breathe again. I've got extra money at the end of the month for the first time in years."

That's what this is about.

Not the house.
Not the rate.
The freedom.

Because when you stop letting interest win—you start taking your life back.

This Rule Is Legal Bank Robbery

> *Let's just say it: mortgages are rigged.*
>
> *They're front-loaded with interest, structured to reward banks, and designed to look friendly while robbing you slowly over 30 years.*

If you don't get aggressive, you'll pay 2 to 2.5 times the amount you borrowed.

That's not an exaggeration. That's how amortization schedules work.

So Rule 11 is about flipping the script.

This chapter is your battle plan for:

- Bi-weekly payments that shave off years
- Small extra payments that create a massive impact
- Prepping for a refinance before the media even reports the drop
- Knowing when not to pay extra
- Creating a payoff plan that's ruthless, smart, and custom to you

We're not playing defense anymore. Let's go.

Let me tell you another story.

A borrower named Mike came to us feeling proud. He'd made every payment for nearly 10 years. Never missed one. Had perfect credit.

But something felt off. He still owed over $290,000 on a $340,000 loan.

We pulled his amortization schedule. Did the math. And that's when Mike saw it: He had paid over $158,000 in total payments so far.

Of that? Only $37,000 had gone to principal. The rest—a whopping $121,000—was pure interest.

Mike went pale.

"Wait, what? I've paid $158K . . . and still owe $290K?" he whispered.

We nodded.

"But . . . I've been doing everything right."

That's the trap.

He followed the bank's rules. He played the game like a good borrower. And the house still won.

Until now.

We showed him a strategy. Just $75 more per month, starting immediately. That alone would cut 6.5 years off his loan and save him $41,000 in interest.

Same loan. Same terms. Same life. Just $2.50 a day redirected.

He set it up that week. And now, three years later, he's knocked almost $15,000 more off the principal than he would have otherwise.

This chapter is about how to do the same.

You're not stuck with the loan the bank gave you.

You can rewrite the ending—if you know the rules.

Destroy the Interest Curve Before It Eats You

Here's the dirty little secret about a 30-year mortgage:

For the first 10 years, you're paying almost all interest.

That $2,800 monthly payment? Maybe $300 goes to principal in year one. The other $2,500+ is profit for the lender.

That's because mortgages are front-loaded. The payment is fixed, but the ratio of interest to principal shifts painfully slowly in your favor.

You don't feel it happening. You see the payment coming out each month and think, "I'm doing the right thing."

But your loan isn't shrinking.

Let's break it down with a hypothetical:

- $400,000 loan at 6.875% interest
- 30-year fixed mortgage
- Monthly payment: ~$2,635 (principal + interest only)

In year 1, you'll pay about $32,000 in total payments. Of that, only $5,400 goes to principal. The remaining $26,600 is pure interest.

Let that sink in. You paid over $30K to live in your house—and only $5K went toward owning it.

By the 10-year mark, you've paid over $320,000 total . . . yet you still owe around $330,000 of your $400K loan.

That's how the system is built.

So what do you do? You get in the ring. You jab back with precision.

How to Weaponize Bi-Weekly Payments

Let's talk about one of the easiest ways to flip the script: Bi-weekly payments.

Sounds boring? Maybe. But it's a ninja-level hack that knocks years off your loan without feeling like you're doing much.

Here's how it works:

- Most people pay their mortgage monthly (12 payments per year)
- If you switch to bi-weekly, you make half a payment every two weeks
- There are 26 pay periods in a year if you get paid bi-weekly
- That means you're making 13 full payments per year, not 12

That single extra payment goes entirely toward principal.

Do it right, and you'll slice 5–7 years off a 30-year mortgage.

Let's run a sample:

- Loan: $400,000 @ 6.875% for 30 years
- Monthly payment: $2,635
- Bi-weekly: $1,317.50 every 2 weeks

Total savings: around $69,000 in interest
Loan payoff: 24.5 years instead of 30

Want to go beast mode?

Add just $50 to every bi-weekly payment. That's $100/month.

Total savings? Could jump to over $90,000 in interest.

One client, Nicole, made just 4 extra half-payments that year. Three years later, she was already over $8,900 ahead on principal.

The best part? It feels invisible. It blends with your normal cash flow.

You won't notice it . . . until you look up and your principal is melting.

Your Mortgage's Worst Nightmare

Let me introduce you to the most powerful financial weapon you probably aren't using: Intentional principal payments.

Every extra dollar you send directly to principal is like throwing a wrench into the lender's profit machine. It's not flashy. It's not sexy. But it's lethal—especially in the first 5 to 10 years of your loan.

Here's the trick:

Even small extra payments early in your loan have an exponential impact.

Why? Because you're punching down the interest curve before it gains momentum.

Say you round up your monthly payment by just $150. That $150, when applied to principal, isn't spread out across your balance. It hits it now—and reduces how much interest is calculated next month.

One client, Jen, added $110/month to her $2,400 mortgage. She shaved nearly 6 years off the loan. Total saved? Over $72,000 in interest.

She didn't refinance.
She didn't restructure her life.
She just added a Starbucks drink and a Chipotle bowl's worth of cash to her payment.

If you can automate it, even better. Set it and forget it. Let your lender or servicer apply the extra principal every month automatically.

The mortgage companies hope you don't know this.

You're not supposed to read the amortization schedule.

They want you numb, compliant, and faithful to the 30-year plan.

But you're in Mortgage Club now. And we don't do numb.

Refinancing Like a Sniper

The next time mortgage rates drop, it'll feel like a frenzy. The media will scream "Time to Refi!" and thousands will jump on the bandwagon.

But the best refinancers are already locked, loaded, and prepped before the headlines hit.

Want to be one of them?

Here's what to do now to be ready for the next window:

1. Keep your credit clean.
   A drop from 702 to 678 could cost you a quarter point in rate. That's thousands lost over the life of the loan. Stay disciplined. Don't open random credit lines. Keep balances under 30%. Pay on time. Every point matters.

2. Have a lender on deck.
   Not just any lender—a sharp one. Someone who can compare wholesale pricing, provide multiple options, and move fast when rates fall. Don't shop during the storm. Build your team during the calm.

3. Know your breakeven.
   A refinance usually comes with closing costs. You need to understand how long it'll take to recoup those costs via lower payments. If it takes 6 years and you'll move in 4, it's probably not worth it. Be strategic.

4. Watch the 10-Year Treasury.
   Mortgage rates move with it. When that yield drops, rates tend to follow. Don't just listen to CNBC. Learn to read the signals yourself. That's how you refi like a sniper.

One of our clients, Sarah, waited too long in 2020. She wanted to "think on it" while rates were at 2.75%. By the time she was ready, they'd jumped back to 3.5%.

She still refinanced . . . but lost out on $12,000 in long-term savings.

Time and interest don't wait.

Build Your Custom Payoff Plan

No two borrowers are alike—so no two payoff plans should be either.

But every smart payoff plan includes the following elements:

- Awareness of your current amortization schedule - Know where you're at. Look at your mortgage statement. Call your lender. Download your full amortization table.
- Your financial margin - How much extra can you realistically apply each month toward principal? $25? $250? $2,000?

- Your timeline and goals – Want to be mortgage-free by retirement? Want to refinance into a 15-year loan? Want to build equity fast to buy a second home?
- Your mortgage type – FHA, VA, USDA, Conventional—each has different refinance options, mortgage insurance rules, and prepayment benefits.

Once you've got the data, here's your move:

1. Set a target date to be mortgage-free.
2. Calculate the monthly principal addition required to hit that target.
3. Automate it. Schedule the overpayment with your servicer.
4. Monitor progress every 6 months. Adjust if needed.

This is your plan. Own it.

Mortgage Club Action Plan

Step 1: Know your amortization.
Get the full schedule. Understand how much interest you're paying this year versus principal. It's your war map.

Step 2: Switch to bi-weekly payments if possible.
One extra payment a year = 5–7 years off your loan = tens of thousands saved.

Step 3: Automate an extra principal payment.

Even $50/month can make a huge dent. Start small and grow it over time.

Step 4: Stay refi-ready.

Monitor your credit. Watch interest rates. Be ready to pounce when the window opens.

Step 5: Build your personal payoff plan.

Set a goal. Pick a date. Create a strategy that fits your lifestyle—and makes you excited to check your mortgage balance.

Final Word

Mortgages are not your enemy.
But interest is.

And the longer you let it win, the more it costs you—not just in dollars, but in peace.

Don't wait for the perfect time.
Don't let your equity grow slower than your Netflix queue.
Don't say "someday" and then blink, and it's been 18 years.

Start now. Start small if you have to.

But whatever you do—start.

Because oncc you take back control of your interest, you take back control of your future.

Welcome to Mortgage Club, Rule 11.

Let's go win this thing.

RULE #12:

Think Like an Investor. Even If You're Not One.

Mortgage Club Confession
"The Bill Method"
– Rich Hanlin

This might be the most important mindset shift in the entire book.

Most people approach homebuying like an emotional roller-coaster—fear of missing out, fear of overpaying, stress about rates, panic over payment. But investors? They walk in with a blueprint. A calm, calculated plan. They make the numbers work for them. And if the deal doesn't pencil out, they walk.

Let me tell you about Bill.

Bill owns over 100 doors—mostly fourplexes. And despite juggling dozens of properties, he's the calmest client I've ever worked with. No drama. No panic. He sends what we need, signs, closes, and moves on to the next one. It's not luck. It's mindset.

Bill never starts with the asking price. He starts with the return.

How much rent does the property bring in? What's the projected monthly cash flow after expenses? What rate can he qualify for, and what loan amount keeps him in the green? From there, he works backward to determine what the property is worth to him. And that's the offer he makes.

If rates go up, his offer goes down. Period. He doesn't care about comps. He's not here to win a bidding war. He's here to win the math.

And here's the kicker—Bill doesn't care what you think your home is worth. He's not being rude. He just knows the numbers don't lie. If the numbers don't work, the deal doesn't happen.

• • • • • • • • • • • • • • •

That's the investor mindset.

And you don't need 100 doors to adopt it. You just need to change your lens. Stop being emotionally manipulated by shiny countertops and granite sinks. Start being driven by logic.

Ask yourself:

- What is my monthly comfort zone?
- What is the ROI (return on investment) on this home?
- How will I win over the long haul?

Because homes are like buses. If you miss this one, another will be by in 15 minutes. And in 36 years, I've never had a single buyer say, "I wish I had gotten that first house." Every single time, they tell me, "Thank God I waited. This one was even better."

Bill taught me something I now teach every client:

The smartest buyer isn't always the one with the most money.
It's the one with the most discipline.

So think like an investor, even if you're not.

This one's not just for the real estate pros or TikTok landlords. This rule is for *everyone.*

Whether you're a school teacher, a first-time buyer, a single mom, or a W-2 employee who's never thought of owning more than your backyard, this rule applies to you:

Think like an investor—even if you're not one.

Because here's the truth: wealth isn't built by accident. It's built with intention. It's built by people who see money not just as income, but as leverage.

And no matter who you are, if you own a home—or plan to—you've already taken the first step into the world of real estate investing. Whether you admit it or not, you're already playing the game.

The question is: are you playing to win?

Equity Is a Tool—Not Just a Gift

Let's get tactical.

When you buy a home, most people think: "Awesome, I now own a $400,000 house."

But if your loan is $380,000, you *don't* own a $400,000 house.

You own $20,000 of it.

The rest? Belongs to the bank.

That doesn't mean you made a mistake. It just means you need to see the *truth* about ownership. Because in that moment, what you really "own" is *equity*—that $20K is your stake in the property.

But equity isn't just a number.

It's power.

It's future options.

It's financial safety.

And most people? They don't treat it like that. They treat it like a number on paper they'll tap *someday*. When they retire. When the kids go to college. When things "calm down."

But we've learned this: the most successful buyers don't just sit on their equity.

They use it. Wisely. Strategically. And unapologetically.

Because in a world where the average American has less than $500 in emergency savings, equity can be the thing that changes the game.

Not credit cards. Not lottery tickets. Not even pay raises.

Equity.

And it's not magic. It's math.

You bought a home for $400,000. You paid down $20K of the loan. And the market jumped 10%.

Congrats. You now have $60,000 in equity.

That's the silent win of real estate.

That's the compounding effect of buying smart.

But again, it only works if you *think* like an investor.

House Hacking: The Gateway Strategy

Let's introduce a strategy that has changed lives, especially for first-time buyers: House Hacking.

Sounds edgy, right? Like a cheat code. Because it kind of is.

House hacking is the idea that your home doesn't just have to be a place you live. It can be a place that *pays you* to live there.

How?

- Rent out a room.
- Rent out the basement.
- Live in one side of a duplex and rent the other.
- Or go big—triplex, fourplex, ADU (we'll get there in a sec).

You don't have to be a landlord in a suit. You just have to be willing to *see your house differently.*

Let's get personal. A family friend of ours bought a 3-bedroom house. He lived in one room, and rented the other two to friends.

They covered two-thirds of his mortgage.

Let that sink in.

He was a homeowner—with roommates—building equity, while his friends paid the bill.

Two years later, the house appreciated by over $150,000.

That's not a fluke. That's the power of using the *home you already live in* as a wealth-building machine.

And here's the beautiful part: FHA and other low-down-payment loans allow you to do this with just 3.5% down—if you *live* in one of the units for a year.

Not forever. Just one year.

Imagine buying a fourplex with 3.5% down...
Living in one unit...
Renting the other three...
And watching your tenants pay off your mortgage while you stack equity.

This isn't get-rich-quick.

This is get-rich-smart.

And it's more possible than most people realize—especially if you're willing to *live simply now to live freely later.*

Let's Talk ADUs

Ever heard of an ADU?

Accessory Dwelling Unit.

It's a small, legally rentable structure on your property—detached, separate, private entrance. Think of it like a little guest house or casita.

It's exploding in popularity in places like California, where rents are insane and space is gold.

People are building ADUs in backyards, side yards, and even converting detached garages. One-bedroom, one-bath, with AC, bathroom, closet—tiny but functional.

Why?

Because you can rent it out for $2,000–$3,000 per month in the right area.

That's not side hustle money. That's mortgage-destroying money.

And here's the kicker: it adds property value, gives you options (rent, Airbnb, family use), and helps you think like an investor *without* having to buy another property.

But it all starts with one question:

What if your home wasn't just a roof over your head—what if it was the key to building freedom?

Your Primary Home Is Leverage, Not Just Shelter

Most people think of their home as a cozy nest.

We want you to think of it as a *launchpad.*

Let's break down a truth that too many homeowners miss:

Your equity is not just wealth—it's leverage.

You don't have to be a real estate tycoon to understand this.

Here's the formula:

- You buy a house.
- You live in it.
- It appreciates.
- You pay down the loan.
- You gain equity.
- You can *use* that equity to go again.

Not to blow it on a boat or Vegas trip.

But to reinvest—into another property, a duplex, a HELOC-powered ADU, or a cashflowing rental.

And here's where it gets wild:

If your home is worth $500,000 and goes up just 4% in a year, that's $20,000 in new equity.

That's 20 grand you didn't *do* anything for.
You slept, paid your mortgage, mowed the lawn . . . and made $20K.

Now do that over 5 years.

Now imagine you used some of that equity to buy another home.

And that one also grew.

This is how regular people—nurses, teachers, military families—become real estate investors.

It's not about getting rich overnight.

It's about *getting richer over time.*

It's about turning your primary home into a *financial engine*—one that can generate wealth long after the furniture is arranged and the family photos are on the wall.

A Quick Reminder from the Math Department

Let's say:

- You bought a $400,000 home.
- It grows 3% annually (pretty conservative).
- That's $12,000 a year in appreciation.
- Meanwhile, you're also paying down the loan (say, $5,000 a year in principal).

That's $17,000 in annual equity growth—without doing anything dramatic.

Now compound that.

And then imagine using that equity to fund your next smart move.

This is how you build generational wealth quietly.

It's not flashy.

It's not TikTok-finance-guru hype.

It's math. It's leverage. It's thinking like an investor—even if you're not one.

"Wealth doesn't come from the house you buy. It comes from how you use the house you bought."

The Quiet Power of House Hacking

Let's break this down practically.

What if you bought a house—not just to live in, but to live in *smarter*?

That's house hacking.

It doesn't require you to be rich, own 10 doors, or know how to calculate cap rates in your sleep.

Here's what it looks like in real life:

- You buy a home.
- You rent out one or two rooms.
- Your roommates pay most (or all) of your mortgage.
- You're living for nearly free—and building equity while you sleep.

This isn't theory. This is what Rich's son did.

Three-bedroom, two-bath house. Rented out two rooms to friends.

Boom—two-thirds of the mortgage covered.

He owned the house for two years.

The home appreciated by over $150,000.

He paid his mortgage.

His roommates covered most of it.

He walked away with a small fortune *before* turning 25.

That's not luck. That's mindset.

The Duplex/Triplex/Fourplex Game

Here's where you level up.

Instead of renting out rooms, you buy a small multi-unit property.

- Duplex.
- Triplex.
- Fourplex.

Live in one unit. Rent out the rest.

What makes this brilliant?

You can still qualify for *owner-occupied financing.*

That means:

Lower rates
Lower down payment
Less cash out of pocket

You're technically buying an investment property . . . but *legally* it's your primary.

Think about that.

You're becoming a landlord without having to be a millionaire.

And in most markets, FHA financing allows you to buy up to a fourplex with as little as 3.5% down—*as long as you live in one unit for at least 12 months.*

You could even move out after a year and rent all the units.

Rinse. Repeat.

Real wealth. Real fast.

Why This Matters—Especially When You're Young

Most people wait too long.

They want the dream home. The granite countertops. The spa tub.

But here's what savvy people do:

They get in early
They live lean
They rent out what they don't need
They reinvest

It's not always glamorous.

You might be sharing a wall.

You might be managing tenants while working a 9-to-5.

But guess what?

Ten years later, you're sitting on multiple properties, a pile of equity, and options most people only dream about.

You bought freedom.

Because you thought like an investor—even when you were "just" a first-time buyer.

The Equity Snowball Strategy

We already talked about building equity and how to leverage your home. But let's go even further—into the advanced game.

Because here's the investor secret:

Equity is meant to move.

It's not just something you sit on like a dragon hoarding gold. It's a tool—and smart investors keep it in motion.

This is what we call **The Equity Snowball Strategy.**

And it's how regular people—schoolteachers, firefighters, couples with average incomes—go from owning one home . . . to five.

What Is the Equity Snowball?

The idea is simple:

1. You buy your first home.
2. You live in it. Improve it. Pay it down. Watch the value rise.

3. Then you **refinance or use a HELOC** to tap into that equity.
4. Use the cash to buy another property.
5. Repeat.

Like a snowball rolling downhill, your real estate portfolio gains momentum.

You don't need to win the lottery. You don't need to save 20% down over and over.

You just need to get the first ball rolling.

Real Life Example: From One to Four

Let's say you bought your first home for $350,000 with 5% down. Three years later, the home is worth $420,000.

You've also paid down your loan by $15,000.

That means you've built roughly **$85,000 in equity.**

You refinance and take out $60,000—leaving a safety cushion.

With that, you put **20% down on a $300,000 rental property.**

That property cash flows $250/month after expenses.

Over the next few years, **both homes appreciate.** You now have even more equity.

You do it again.

That's the equity snowball.

Why It Works

Because real estate grows in two directions:

1. **Downward:** As you pay down the loan.
2. **Upward:** As the home appreciates.

Equity is the gap in between.

And when you tap into that equity to buy more assets, you're leveraging growth.

It's **compound interest meets real estate.**

The Risks (Let's Be Smart)

We're not saying pull every dollar of equity and buy 5 condos in Vegas.

You need to:

Buy in good markets
Understand cash flow
Have reserves

Stress test your strategy
Know your limits

A snowball works best when you're **in control.**

This isn't HGTV flipping fantasies. This is a long-term, wealth-building strategy.

Advanced Tip: BRRRR Strategy

Ever heard of BRRRR?

Buy. Rehab. Rent. Refinance. Repeat.

This is next-level snowballing.

You buy an undervalued home. You fix it up. You rent it. Then you refinance it based on the new value. Pull the cash out—and do it again.

It's not for everyone. But it's how investors multiply.

Mindset Shift: Your Home Isn't a Destination

Most people think they're "done" once they buy a home. But the wealthy see that home as just the beginning.

It's a launchpad.

The first domino.

A stepping stone to something bigger.

Even if you don't want 10 rentals or to become a landlord, the mindset matters.

Because when you **see equity as fuel**, you realize you're sitting on untapped power.

And that's what separates average homeowners from strategic ones.

Plan Your Next Move (Without Getting Stuck in Analysis Paralysis)

Let's get one thing out of the way:

You do not need to know your "forever plan" to make your next move.

Too many people get stuck in real estate because they're overthinking it:

"What if I want to move in 7 years?"
"What if rates change?"
"What if the market dips?"

Guess what?

All of that might happen.
And you'll still be okay—if you understand the fundamentals.

The key isn't predicting the future.
It's **positioning yourself to have options.**

Option = Freedom

Let's say you:

Buy smart
Build equity
Keep your payments manageable
Don't overextend

Then you've already set yourself up for success—no matter what happens.

Because equity gives you:

- The option to sell
- The option to refinance
- The option to rent it out
- The option to stay and pay it off
- The option to turn it into a stepping stone for the next property

You're not trapped. You're **empowered.**

But you can't play the game from the sideline.

At some point, you have to **move.**

How to Plan Your Next Move

Here's a dead-simple framework we give our clients:

1. **What's your 3-year lifestyle goal?**
   - o Bigger yard?
   - o Better schools?
   - o Lower payments?
   - o Work-from-home space?

2. **What's your 10-year financial goal?**
   - o Build equity?
   - o Own rentals?
   - o Retire early?
   - o Pay off the mortgage?

3. **What can you do today that moves both needles?**

That's the magic intersection.

You're not just reacting.
You're playing chess.

You're living smart **now**, while setting up wins for later.

We've Seen This in Action

There was a client—let's call her Monica.
Single mom, two kids, working full-time as a nurse.

She didn't think she could ever buy a home.
Until she realized she had enough for 3% down on a townhome.

She bought it.
Two years later, it appreciated $70,000.
She refinanced, pulled cash, and used it for a duplex down payment.

She rented out the townhome and moved into the duplex.
Now? Her old home cashflows $600/month.
And she's got equity in both places.

All because she **moved once.**

The Rule of 1 and Done

Here's something we tell all new buyers:

"Don't worry about owning five homes. Own one—and own it well."

You don't need a real estate empire.
You just need to make your **first move** a smart one.

If that leads to a second property? Great.
If it just gives you financial stability? That's a win, too.

Because either way, you're no longer watching from the sidelines.

You're **in the game.**

The Investor Mindset Starts Now

Alright. You made it.

Twelve rules. Dozens of stories. Probably a few moments where your brain exploded in the best possible way.

And here we are—Rule 12.

This is the final push. But it might just be the **most important** mindset of all.

Because everything you've learned comes down to this:

You don't need to be a real estate tycoon. You just need to think like one.

Your Home Is a Wealth Engine

It's not just shelter.

It's not just a mortgage.

It's a **wealth-generating machine**—if you know how to use it.

And once you understand that equity is power, appreciation is leverage, and ownership equals options... You can't unsee it.

You start looking at every home—yours, your neighbor's, that one across town—as an opportunity.

A chess piece.

A tool.

Investor Thinking in Everyday Life

Investor thinking is about **calculated moves**.

It's not risky. It's strategic.

You don't need to have 100 doors like Bill. But if you approach decisions like he does, you start winning:

- Asking: *What can this asset do for me next?*
- Looking at ROI instead of just price tags
- Thinking in decades, not weekends
- Valuing liquidity, leverage, and long-game positioning

You don't need to act like you're on CNBC.
Just start asking better questions when it comes to real estate.

That alone will change your life.

Your Action Plan

Let's leave you with something tangible:

Step 1: Know Your Numbers

- What's your home worth today?
- What do you owe?
- What's your equity?
- Could you refinance or get a HELOC?
- What's your DTI (debt-to-income) ratio?

Step 2: Define Your Next Move

- Refi and renovate?
- Buy a second home or a rental?
- House hack?
- Sell and trade up?
- Stay put—but pay it down faster?

Step 3: Get Mentors

Find 1–2 people in your life who've made good real estate moves.
Ask them to coffee. Take notes. Learn from them.

(And if you don't know any? Congrats—you've got *us*. Seriously.)

Step 4: Take One Step

Even if it's just checking your equity.
Even if it's just setting a goal to buy in 18 months.

Start the momentum.

Mortgage Club Was Never Just About Mortgages

This book? These rules?

It wasn't really about interest rates or credit scores or disclosures.

It was about something bigger:

It was about control.

Control over your decisions.
Control over your finances.
Control over your future.

Mortgages were just the language we used to teach it.

But now you know what most people don't.

You know the playbook.

And more importantly?

You know how to think like an investor—even if you're not one.

CONCLUSION

You're One of Us Now.

Let's be honest.
You probably didn't pick up this book thinking it would change your life.
Maybe a friend handed it to you.
Maybe you saw it on Instagram next to some meme about avocado toast and 8% interest rates.
Or maybe your lender said, "Hey, you should read this before you sign your life away."

We get it.
It's called *Mortgage Club*, not *Eat, Pray, Loan.*

But here's the twist: this isn't just a book about mortgages. This is a book about ownership—not just of property, but of your choices, your financial future, your mindset.

And ownership, when done right, changes everything.

You Made It Through All 12 Rules

You survived the fight.
You dodged the fees. You blocked the bad advice.
You landed a few punches of your own—maybe even scored a knockout by negotiating a better deal.

And if you read every chapter?
You're not a rookie anymore.
You're not just "approved." You're informed.
You're not just signing papers. You're signing with confidence.

You now know more than 90% of buyers out there.
And that . . . is dangerous—in the best way possible.

So What Happens Now?

Here's what we want you to know before we part ways:
You're allowed to own your future.
You're allowed to make bold decisions about where you live, what you invest in, and what you build for your family.
You don't have to wait for perfect timing, permission, or some government program to save you.

You've got the playbook now. You can go back and read any chapter as needed.
You've got the blueprint.
The battle-tested wisdom of two guys who've walked hundreds of families through the fire and out the other side.
You know how to spot the trap.
You know when someone's "pitching" you.
You know what real financial power looks like.

This Was Always Bigger Than a Loan

If all we did was help you save $3,500 in lender fees, cool.
If you finished this book and said, "Yeah, I'm going to shop smarter," great.

But that was never the real mission.

We wrote this because we believe in something bigger:

- **Homeownership is a path to freedom**.
- Smart lending is how families **escape the paycheck-to-paycheck cycle**.
- Knowing your numbers is the fastest way to **get unstuck**.
- And confidence? That's built, not given. You can't outsource confidence. You build it by learning, doing, and staying in the fight.

The American Lie (And the Truth About Wealth)

There's this lie that gets whispered in our ears from the time we're kids.
It goes something like this:

"Go to school. Get good grades. Get a good job. Buy a nice house. Stay in your lane. Retire at 65. Then, finally, you can relax."

And you know what?
A lot of people follow that formula—and end up stressed, stretched thin, and scared to check their bank account.

Because the truth is: wealth was never about just working hard.

We've seen it.

Buyers who make $300K a year . . . but spend $310K.

Doctors drowning in student loans.

Successful couples in nice neighborhoods . . . stuck in quiet financial panic.

And then we've seen the opposite.

Buyers with modest incomes . . . who planned. Who learned. Who leveraged.

They became millionaires.

Not because of luck.

Not because of inheritance.

But because they understood the real math of ownership.

Owning Smart Beats Owning Big

We say it all the time:

"It's not how much house you can qualify for. It's how much house you can afford to enjoy."

Big homes don't build wealth. Smart mortgages do.

Nobody posts pictures of their 30-year amortization schedule on Instagram.

But if they did?

The smart ones would be flexing those bi-weekly payments, seller credits, and no-fee refis.

Because that's where the wealth is.

In the quiet, consistent, well-informed choices.

Don't Buy Into the Flash. Buy Into the Freedom.

You'll see ads. You'll hear coworkers. You'll get pressure.
"Go bigger."
"Stretch for it."
"You can always refinance later."
"Live a little."

But here's our advice:

Live a lot. Later.
Live free.
Live with margin.
Live with choices.
Not chained to a house payment that leaves you one car repair away from crisis.
Own the home. Don't let the home own you.

What Wealth Really Feels Like (Spoiler: It's Not What You Think)

Let's set the record straight.
Wealth doesn't feel like popping champagne on a yacht. (Okay, maybe sometimes it does. But that's not the everyday version.)

Wealth feels like sleeping soundly on a Thursday night because your mortgage is dialed in.
It feels like pulling into your driveway and knowing—you own this.

Not the bank. Not your landlord.
Not your cousin's old roommate who just raised your rent.

It feels like options.
Like not sweating the water heater repair.
Like saying yes to your kid's field trip without checking the credit card balance first.

Real wealth is boring.
And that's the best kind.
It's the kind where your net worth grows quietly in the background while you're eating spaghetti with your family.

The Power of Predictable

If we could give every buyer one gift, it wouldn't be a lower interest rate.
It would be a sense of control.

Because when your housing payment is predictable, your life becomes intentional.
You stop living reactively.
You start playing offense.
You're not worried about market crashes or landlord surprises or inflation gut punches.

Because you have a plan.
You're locked in. You're leveraged right. You're liquid.

You're lean.
That's wealth.

Don't Just Buy a House. Build a Future.

A mortgage isn't a finish line.
It's a foundation.

It's the platform you build everything else on—family, finances, freedom, legacy.

This book wasn't about being "good at loans."
It's about being dangerously smart with your biggest life purchase.

Because once your mortgage is handled?
You can go build the life you were actually meant to live.

Lessons from the Buyers Who Got It Right (and a Few Who Got It Really Wrong)

Let's take a minute and talk about the humans.
You know, the people behind the credit scores and W-2s.

Because behind every mortgage is a heartbeat.

We've had buyers who brought spreadsheets to the pre-approval meeting.
And buyers who brought Starbucks and just said, "So . . . what's a mortgage?"

We've helped widows rebuild.
Young couples dream big.
Families relocate, restart, and rise.

And through it all, we've learned this:
The mortgage doesn't define the buyer.
But the buyer absolutely defines the mortgage.

Story: The Couple Who Read the Book

They were in their early 30s. Not high-income. Just smart.

They came in one day, sat down, and dropped a printed copy of one of our YouTube transcripts on the table.

"Rule 4," they said. "Choose your loan type. We read it twice. We're not doing FHA."

(We knew right then—we were gonna get along just fine.)

They picked a strategy, asked sharp questions, and negotiated seller credits like pros.

They closed early, moved in, and nine months later, sent us a photo of the baby they'd been waiting to have until things felt stable.

That's the magic.
Not the rate.
Not the closing gift.
But the confidence they carried into their next chapter.

Story: The Borrower Who Waited Too Long

On the other end of the spectrum: we had a guy, mid-40s, good job, credit in the high 700s.
But he couldn't pull the trigger.

Rates went up? He waited.
Prices dipped? He waited more.
His lease renewed? He waited again.

Over the course of two years, he watched as:

- His rent increased twice
- The home he liked sold to someone else
- Rates ticked up 1.5%

He finally bought.
But he overpaid, under-leveraged, and missed out on thousands in appreciation.

Why?

Because fear whispered louder than strategy.
He didn't think like an investor.
He thought like someone hoping the perfect deal would fall in his lap.
Spoiler: It didn't.

A home isn't just where you live. It's where your future grows roots.

Smart Buyers Aren't Perfect. They're Proactive.

You don't need to nail every move.
You just need to move with intention.

The best buyers?
They're not always the ones with the biggest budgets.
They're the ones who:

- Ask questions
- Listen with curiosity
- Build relationships with their lender
- Think long-term
- Take action even when it's uncomfortable

That's the heartbeat of *Mortgage Club.*
Not perfection.
Precision and participation.

And that brings us to what might be the most important truth of this whole book...

The Most Important Truth of All

Here it is.
The whole secret, if there even is one:

This mortgage isn't just about the house. It's about who you become in the process.

That might sound dramatic.
But we've seen it.

People come into this journey one way—and leave changed. Not just with a home. But with:

- More confidence
- More clarity
- More conviction in their financial life

Because once you've stared down the mortgage jungle and made it out the other side?

You're not just a borrower anymore.

You're a homeowner.
A strategist.
A person who reads fine print, makes data-driven moves, and knows how to pivot under pressure.
You're someone who knows your worth—and won't overpay for it.

This Book Wasn't About the Rules

Okay . . . it was a little bit about the rules.
But more than that?
It was about giving you back your power.

Because most people are out here thinking the lender is in charge.
The system. The bank. The credit score algorithm. The underwriter with a bad attitude.

But not you.
You read 12 chapters of underground, uncensored, unfiltered mortgage truth.
You learned how to flip the script.
How to get in the driver's seat.
How to never get played again.

And most importantly?
You learned that you're not alone.

A Message from Us to You

Let us break character for a second.
This isn't "Coach Rich" and "Professor Tim" talking to you about funding timelines or rate sheets.

This is just two guys who've sat across the table from thousands of people for almost four decades—some hopeful, some terrified, some one signature away from tears—and we're telling you:

You did good.
You made it through.
You read a book that wasn't written to impress anyone.
It was written to protect you.
To wake you up.
To keep you from becoming just another statistic in a business that too often forgets there's a real human behind every FICO score.

We've watched people cry at the closing table.
We've watched people freeze up during pre-approvals because they thought they'd be judged.
We've seen buyers go from broke and broken to building equity, confidence, and generational wealth—just by having the right strategy and the right support.

So we wrote this book to be that support.
To be that strategy in your back pocket.

We don't have perfect lives, but we've helped people buy homes through divorces, layoffs, relocations, funerals, and complete chaos.
And we've learned one thing:

Smart mortgage moves = peace of mind.

That's what we want for you.
We want your dinner table conversations to be about vacations and memories—not whether you're going to

make the mortgage this month because your lender gave you a payment you couldn't sustain.

We want your kids to see what stability looks like.
We want you to feel proud every time you pull into the driveway.
And maybe, just maybe, we want you to come back and work with us again when you're ready to make your next move—because people like you? You're exactly why we still do this.

The Last Word

Let's land this plane with the truth.

You don't have to be rich to build wealth.
You don't have to be a genius to make smart moves.
You don't have to "wait for the market to be perfect" to start.

You just need the guts to begin.
You need the nerve to ask questions.
The wisdom to slow down.
The courage to say, "I deserve better than the status quo."

That's why *Mortgage Club* exists.
Because the mortgage world is noisy. And shady. And weird.
And in the middle of all that noise, we wanted to give you a flashlight.

Something bright. Something honest. Something that says: "Hey. You're not crazy for wanting to understand this stuff."

You're not crazy for wanting to negotiate.
To shop your rate.
To ask what that lender fee actually is.
To question why someone wants to shove you into a loan type that doesn't match your goals.

You're not crazy for wanting to think like an investor—even if you've never owned a single property.
You're not crazy for wanting to protect your money, your future, your peace of mind.
You're not crazy for wanting to be free.

So Go, Be Free

Go own your decisions.
Own your loan.
Own your power.
Own your story.

This isn't just about a house.
This is about the version of you that walks taller because you did it the right way.

You outsmarted the game.
You joined the club.

You didn't just buy a home—
You bought into your future.

And if nobody else told you this yet, let us be the first:
We're proud of you.

Welcome to *Mortgage Club.*
Now go win some deals.

- Rich & Tim

www.ingramcontent.com/pod-product-compliance
Lightning Source LLC
LaVergne TN
LVHW022157200926
848481LV00006B/1774
9798349557354